Cowtown Comfort

CELESTINA BLOK

REEDY PRESS

Reedy Press
PO Box 5131
St. Louis, MO, 63139, USA
reedypress.com

LOC: 2024948768
ISBN: 9781681065762

Printed in Canada
26 27 28 29 5 4 3 2

TABLE OF CONTENTS

INTRODUCTION

Picture this: A newcomer to Fort Worth asks you to describe the city's food scene. Also, why do people call Fort Worth "Cowtown?"

The answers go hand-in-hand.

Between the 1880s and 1950s, Fort Worth reigned as the largest livestock-trading center in the Southwest, fueled by the ease of transporting cattle thanks to the Texas & Pacific Railway. The city became known as "Cowtown," and the moniker stuck. The hub for all this cattle exchanging was the Fort Worth Stockyards, today a historic district that preserves the cowboy culture of the past with daily cattle drives and year-round rodeos.

Naturally, beef is big in Fort Worth, woven into the city's food culture organically more than a century ago. Steaks, barbecue, and burgers might be considered three of Fort Worth's four main food groups, and this book covers them all in great detail.

The fourth? Tex-Mex. Here's a little 101.

Tex-Mex cuisine was born from blending Mexican and American cooking traditions and originated in southern Texas around the Rio Grande Valley in the late 1800s. The concept is identified by signature ingredients like ground beef, yellow cheese, and flour tortillas. (Read more on page 43)

But the food-lovers here know Cowtown cuisine is much more wide-ranging than just steak, brisket, and fajitas. A few examples: The city is home to several Italian eateries with chefs who simmer scratch-made sauces and make pasta in-house. Asian food is huge, with endless options for authentic Vietnamese, Thai, Lao, Japanese, and Chinese fare. There's also a massive market for artfully presented, upscale contemporary cuisine.

While this book is called Cowtown Comfort, know that the recipes showcased here are not restricted to the traditional definition of "comfort food." In this case, the term refers to that comforting feeling of familiarity in enjoying food in Fort Worth. Cutting into a perfectly grilled ribeye. Ladling a spoon into warm tortilla soup. Slicing a freshly baked buttermilk pie. It's a feeling of being home, whether you're new to the city or a lifelong native, and dining at your favorite restaurant or grilling in your own backyard.

Cheers to Cowtown cuisine. Let the cooking begin.

SPECIAL TOOLS, INGREDIENTS, AND TERMS

Cooking in a restaurant kitchen is not like cooking at home. Many professional chefs have staff who will prepare bulk ingredients in advance, like bins of chopped onions, pots of premade stocks, and pounds of shredded chicken. They also have access to commercial equipment not typical for home use. The recipes in the following pages have been modified as "home versions," but there are a few unique tools required, as well as some special lingo, that need to be reviewed.

BLENDER

Several recipes in this book call for blending sauces and soups for a restaurant-style presentation. A handheld immersion blender or high-powered blender will come in handy.

CAST IRON SKILLET

The time-honored heavy pan is essential for authentic Cowtown cooking at home and for many of the recipes listed in this book.

CHICKEN BASE

A concentrated chicken flavoring made of roasted chicken and spices, this special ingredient is a step up from the basic bouillon.

COCKTAIL SHAKER

Used by bartenders to shake up libations in professional fashion.

COOKING THERMOMETER

Required for determining heat of oil for frying and level of doneness for proteins. If investing in one tool for these recipes, make it this one.

DOUGHNUT CUTTER

There are two recipes in this book that require this special tool for the most professional presentation.

FRYER

Frying is big in Fort Worth cooking, whether it's chicken fried steak, chicken fried oysters, fried doughnuts, or even Indian fry bread. A deep fryer is not required but could be considered more convenient than a deep pan filled with oil.

PEPPERS

Prepare to be schooled on peppers throughout this book as many recipes call for some piquancy. Get to know your local Mexican market or make a visit to Pendery's World of Chiles & Spices, one of Cowtown's oldest businesses.

STAND MIXER

Cooking enthusiasts know a stand mixer can make all the difference when it comes to creating pasta and certain types of dough. If a mixer has been hiding deep in a cabinet, now is the time to pull it out.

"TO TASTE"

Listed next to certain seasonings like salt and pepper in many recipes, the term "to taste" can be daunting for those who prefer an exact measurement. When this term is listed, it simply means to add that particular ingredient to your liking. Starting in small quantities is best before "tasting" to test, then adding more if desired.

Photo courtesy of Clearfork Farmers Market

ACKNOWLEDGMENTS

Thank you for picking up this book, flipping through its story-telling pages, and capturing a glimpse of the many flavors of Fort Worth.

Those closest to me know I love to eat—a lot. For me, a meal is a chance to make a memory, create or keep a tradition, reconnect with friends and family, or celebrate a blessing. Great food is the icing on the cake . . . or the gravy on the chicken fried steak. (Or the queso on a tortilla chip. I could go on.)

Having written hundreds of articles covering food news in Fort Worth for 20 years—from restaurant happenings and recipe stories to chef tips and cocktail roundups—I fathomed that writing a cookbook might be in the cards one day. I envisioned the book as a collection of delicious dishes from Cowtown, my place of birth as a third-generation native.

The opportunity presented itself sooner than anticipated, and after a year of gathering, editing, testing, and photographing recipes from 60 different Fort Worth restaurants, eateries, bakeries, and chefs, the finished product now sits in your hands. Thank you, Reedy Press, for giving me a chance on this project and being patient with me along the way.

Please consider this a love letter to our great city, one that illustrates Fort Worth's food culture while showcasing the immense culinary talent that exists here.

This book certainly would not be possible without the food lovers that helped create it, including every single restaurant owner, chef, and baker I asked to share a recipe. They handed over their tried-and-true methods, not asking for anything in return. I hope that you will dive into their dishes and realize the amount of time and dedication that goes into creating each. I also hope you will patronize their establishments to appreciate their culinary ability firsthand.

Thank you also to my dear friends who love to be in the kitchen, including my mom. Every recipe in this book is an "at-home" version that needed to be tested, and so many folks enthusiastically threw on their aprons, pulled out their measuring cups, and raised their hands to help.

Thank you especially to Crystal Vastine and Lauren Cook, both longtime friends and fellow graduates of the Culinary School of Fort Worth. Crystal incorporated recipe testing into her meal planning and even coordinated dinner parties featuring many of these dishes. (Follow her on Instagram @fwfoodie for the latest on the local food scene.) Lauren, a culinary talent on her own, is a private chef who tested several recipes and even beautifully staged and photographed them. See her own delicious recipes at whiskandshake.com.

While the book makes for a great coffee table conversation piece, I hope you will flip through its pages with flour-dusted fingers while actually using it. Make flour tortillas to take to a friend. Surprise the family with German pancakes on Saturday morning. Or plan for a big pot of pozole for your next holiday dinner party. Share these local flavors and eat well.

Love,
Celestina Blok

Photo courtesy of Visit Fort Worth

Taco Heads

COWTOWN COCKTAILS

A great meal often starts with a good cocktail, which is why this chapter is listed first.

While an icy frozen schooner filled with frothy cold beer might be most popular in Fort Worth, the almighty margarita reigns as queen of the cocktail category. Multiple versions exist on every menu in town, from skinny and spicy to fruity and frozen.

Narratives vary on the margarita's origin, with some saying the lime-based libation was invented in El Paso in 1942 and others promising it was born on the Texas coast in Galveston in 1948. It was likely created earlier in Mexico (where tequila is made), with some stories basing the drink out of Acapulco and others saying it was Puebla.

Regardless of origin, you'll find a high-quality version here from Taco Heads, a local taco bar and restaurant whose founder, Sarah Castillo, is also co-founder of a tequila brand called La Pulga. Use it, along with fresh lime juice (never a mix), to create an authentic Cowtown rendition of the popular concoction.

Speaking of tequila, the spirit is super popular in Fort Worth. Other common tequila-based cocktails here include the Ranch Water, a more recent phenomenon with west Texas roots, and the trendy, grapefruit juice-based Paloma.

Any roundup of Fort Worth cocktails should also include a version of the classic old fashioned, and Blackland Distillery is a leader in crafting them. The local distillery and cocktail bar offers several versions, including one with pecan and brown sugar-infused bourbon featured in this book.

Fort Worth's first distillery is TX Whiskey Ranch, opened in 2012. Locals call the distillery's signature spirit simply TX. Any cocktail using it, be it a whiskey sour or a hot toddy, is always a win.

For measuring purposes on the following recipes, note that a standard shot glass is 1½ ounces.

MARIA'S TOP SHELF MARGARITA—*TACO HEADS*

Makes 1 serving

Fort Worth's signature cocktail is, no doubt, the margarita. There's a version of the tequila-based, lime juice-shaken libation on every bar menu in town, from the trendiest destinations to the most divey cantinas. Consider this version, made with Fort Worth-based La Pulga Tequila, a go-to for a standard rendition of the beloved classic.

INGREDIENTS

1 lime wedge

margarita salt for rim, as needed

1 ½ ounces La Pulga Tequila Reposado

juice from 1 lime

½ ounce Cointreau orange liqueur

½ ounce Agave Simple Syrup (recipe follows)

DIRECTIONS

1. Prepare margarita glass by sweeping rim with lime wedge, then dipping into margarita salt to coat rim. Fill with ice.
2. In a cocktail shaker also filled with ice, combine tequila, lime juice, Cointreau, and simple syrup. Shake vigorously and strain into prepared glass. Garnish with lime wedge if desired.

AGAVE SIMPLE SYRUP

Yield: 1 cup

INGREDIENTS

½ cup agave nectar

½ cup hot water

DIRECTIONS

Combine agave nectar and hot water, and stir until agave dissolves. Let cool completely before using. May be stored in the refrigerator for up to 1 month.

Photo courtesy of Adrian Cortes

RANCH WATER—*HOTEL DROVER*

Makes 1 serving

Skyrocketing in popularity in recent years, the Ranch Water is said to have originated in west Texas. Named for the ranchers who drank it to keep cool, it's fitting a Fort Worth Stockyards hotel that honors ranch life shakes up one of the best in town. Purists might skip the simple syrup, but the effervescent Topo Chico is required.

INGREDIENTS

1 lime wedge

Tajín Clásico Seasoning, as needed for rimming glass

1 ½ ounces Casamigos Tequila Blanco

½ ounce freshly squeezed lime juice

¼ ounce simple syrup

1 bottle Topo Chico Mineral Water, chilled

DIRECTIONS

1. Prepare a tall glass by sweeping rim with lime wedge, then dipping into Tajín to coat rim. Fill with ice.
2. In a cocktail shaker also filled with ice, combine tequila, lime juice, and simple syrup. Shake and strain into prepared glass. Top with Topo Chico and garnish with lime wedge.

MEXICO CITY PALOMA—*PALOMA SUERTE*

Makes 1 serving

This grapefruit-forward concoction, which originated in Mexico City cantinas, is a refreshing alternative to the margarita and very on-trend in upscale Mexican restaurants like Tim Love's Paloma Suerte. This version is true to its Mexican roots with the use of Squirt, but club soda may be substituted for a less sweet option.

INGREDIENTS

1 ½ ounces tequila blanco

1 lime

3 to 4 grapefruit quarters, plus more if needed

Squirt grapefruit soda, for topping off

sea salt, for garnish

lime wheel, for garnish

DIRECTIONS

Fill a 16-ounce glass with ice and add tequila. Juice the lime and grapefruit quarters over the ice. When the juices reach about an inch below the mouth of the glass, top off with Squirt and stir. Sprinkle beverage with sea salt and garnish with lime wheel.

THE BOOTSTITCH—*TX WHISKEY RANCH*

Makes 1 serving

Fort Worth's first whiskey distillery debuted in 2012, forever changing the spirits scene in Cowtown. TX Whiskey Ranch is now touted as the largest distillery west of the Mississippi, spanning more than 100 acres. This fan-favorite cocktail from TX Whiskey's lead mixologist combines citrus and Texas flair with a jalapeno kick.

INGREDIENTS

2 fresh jalapeno slices (reserve 1 for garnish)
½ ounce agave nectar
½ ounce lime juice
2 ounces TX Blended Whiskey
1 ounce grapefruit juice
1 rosemary sprig (optional)

DIRECTIONS

In a cocktail shaker, muddle 1 jalapeno slice with agave nectar and lime juice. Add whiskey and grapefruit juice and shake. Strain into highball glass filled with ice and garnish with remaining jalapeno slice and rosemary sprig, if desired. Torch sprig briefly until smoky to enhance flavors before serving.

SALTED PECAN OLD FASHIONED—*BLACKLAND DISTILLERY*

Makes 1 serving

Here's a Fort Worth spin on a bourbon classic from a local distillery that's popular for its lineup of innovative spirits. The result is a pecan-infused, brown sugar-kissed cocktail that's balanced with spice from traditional rye whiskey. A pinch of salt pulls it all together.

INGREDIENTS

1 ounce Blackland Texas Pecan Brown Sugar Bourbon

1 ounce Blackland Rye Whiskey

2 to 3 dashes of black walnut bitters

1 pinch of salt

1 candied pecan, for garnish (found at Vending Nut Company or any gourmet grocer)

DIRECTIONS

Add all ingredients, except pecan, to a mixing glass filled with ice. Stir to chill and slightly dilute. Strain into a cocktail glass with a fat ice cube. Garnish with candied pecan.

Garlic-Stuffed Beef Tenderloin,
Lonesome Dove Western Bistro

STEAKHOUSE & FANCY

FORT WORTH DISHES

Fort Worth's rich history as a hub for cattle trading contributes to its designation as a top spot for steaks. Visit the Fort Worth Stockyards, where all that livestock exchanging took place a century ago, and diners will find more than a half-dozen steakhouses within steps of each other.

One of those is Lonesome Dove Western Bistro, where chef Tim Love elevated Fort Worth's steak game with inventive selections like Wagyu tomahawk and elk ribeye when he opened the fine dining destination in 2000. He shares a recipe here for a more accessible garlic-stuffed beef tenderloin one can make at home.

Undoubtedly, opinions on steaks are strong in Fort Worth. From cuts to cook time, there's a lot to consider. Cook it too long and the steak could taste like a shoe. If the steak is too chilled before being grilled, uneven cooking is likely.

The experts at The Meat Board, an independent Fort Worth butcher shop with high-end cuts of beef, share their tips here on how best to prepare the classic ribeye steak, perhaps Fort Worth's most popular cut. Always start with good quality beef, bring it to room temperature, and the rest is pretty simple.

Other recipes featured in this chapter are considered "Fort Worth Fancy." Guests are going to arrive a little dressier when dining at the establishments from which they originate. The recipes are going to require a little more prep work in advance and finesse in finishing. The result is a visually appealing dish with many facets of flavor. These recipes might be saved for more elaborate dinner gatherings. All showcase what "Fort Worth Fancy" entails on a plate, like Texas Shrimp & Grits from Bonnell's Fine Texas Cuisine, Chicken Fried Texas Oysters with Chipotle Butter & Mango Pico from 97 West Kitchen & Bar, and the immensely popular Toad in a Hole salad dressed with Truffle Vinaigrette from Grace.

TOAD IN A HOLE—*GRACE*

Makes 4 servings

A play on the entertainingly named comfort food classic, Grace's buttery brioche-based Toad in a Hole is one of the downtown fine dining destination's most popular menu items. The luxurious white truffle vinaigrette adds a level of decadence for which chef Blaine Staniford is known.

INGREDIENTS

4 slices brioche

unsalted butter, as needed

4 eggs

sea salt and pepper, to taste

1 bunch frisee chicory, washed and trimmed

1 pound wild arugula, washed and trimmed

1 bunch asparagus, blanched and chopped

Pickled Red Onion (recipe follows)

Truffle Vinaigrette (recipe follows)

½ pound bacon slices, fried and cut in half

DIRECTIONS

1. Using a doughnut cutter, cut the center of each slice of brioche.
2. Heat a medium-size sauté pan over medium heat. Add enough butter to coat the bottom of the pan. Place brioche "doughnuts" into the pan and crack an egg onto the center of each. Reduce the heat to low and cook until egg white has set. Using an offset spatula, flip over each brioche slice and cook other side until golden brown and egg white has fully set, making sure egg yolk is still runny. Season with salt and pepper and keep warm.
3. In a stainless steel bowl, combine frisee, arugula, asparagus, and Pickled Red Onion. Season with salt and pepper, to taste. Pour desired amount of Truffle Vinaigrette over greens and lightly toss until well coated.
4. Divide salad mixture among 4 plates and top each with a brioche slice and 3 to 4 bacon slices. Serve warm.

PICKLED RED ONION

INGREDIENTS

1 red onion, sliced

1 cup red wine vinegar

½ cup red wine

¼ cup granulated sugar

DIRECTIONS

1. Place all ingredients in a medium-size pot over high heat. Bring to a boil.
2. Remove from heat and place pot into a bowl filled with ice water until cooled.
3. Once cooled, place onions in airtight container and keep in refrigerator. Pickled onions will keep for 1 month in refrigerator.

TRUFFLE VINAIGRETTE

Yield: ½ cup

INGREDIENTS

½ cup white truffle oil

2 tablespoons peanut oil

1 shallot, minced

1 garlic clove, minced

1 lemon, juiced

sea salt and pepper, to taste

DIRECTIONS

Mix all ingredients together in a stainless steel bowl, seasoning to desired taste with salt and pepper. Place in airtight container. Vinaigrette will keep in refrigerator for about a week.

HOMEGROWN TOMATO & MASCARPONE TART—*ELLERBE FINE FOODS*

Makes 8 servings

A pioneer in Fort Worth farm-to-table dining, Ellerbe Fine Foods has been recognized by *Bon Appetit* magazine and the James Beard Foundation. Chef Molly McCook still regularly visits local farmers markets for her ingredients and recommends serving this recipe with a simple arugula salad dressed with lemon juice and extra virgin olive oil.

INGREDIENTS

2 cups all-purpose flour, plus more for work surface

1 teaspoon kosher salt, divided

1 stick unsalted butter, chilled

1 egg

2 tablespoons cold water

⅓ cup mascarpone cheese

1 tablespoon fresh thyme, chopped

1 large homegrown tomato, sliced ¼ inch thick

2 green tomatoes, sliced ¼ inch thick

¼ teaspoon fresh ground black pepper

zest of 1 lemon

Photo courtesy of Lauren Cook

DIRECTIONS

1. To make the crust, combine flour and ½ teaspoon salt in a bowl. Cut the butter into the flour using a fork or fingers until the mixture is the consistency of cornmeal.
2. In a separate small bowl, whisk together the egg and water. Make a well in the center of the flour mixture and pour the liquid into the center. Work the flour mixture and liquid together to form dough.
3. Lightly flour a work surface and roll the dough out to approximately ½ inch thickness. Transfer the dough to an 8-inch tart pan with a removable bottom, or onto a cookie sheet. If using a tart pan, the dough should come up the sides of the pan approximately 1 inch.
4. Heat oven to 425 degrees.
5. Spread the bottom of the dough with mascarpone cheese. (Leave a 1-inch border if not using a tart pan.) Sprinkle with chopped thyme.
6. Sprinkle the sliced tomatoes with pepper and remaining salt, pat dry, and then layer over the mascarpone, alternating the red and green. Sprinkle lemon zest over the tomatoes.
7. Gently fold the edges of the tart dough over the corners of the tomatoes to form a crust. Bake approximately 25 to 30 minutes or until the crust is golden brown. Remove from oven and gently drain the excess liquid. Let sit for 5 minutes before slicing into 8 portions.

Photo courtesy of
Clearfork Farmers Market

GRILLED ARTICHOKES WITH LEMON AIOLI—*TAVERN*

Makes 4-6 servings

This fan-favorite appetizer at one of Fort Worth's most popular neighborhood restaurants is always a crowd pleaser thanks to its smoky char that comes from a final grill over a wood-burning fire. Steaming first and serving with a perky aioli is the key to a successful rendition made at home.

INGREDIENTS

3 globe artichokes

olive oil, as needed for brushing artichokes

½ lemon

DIRECTIONS

1. Cut 1 inch off each artichoke stem. Using a vegetable peeler or paring knife, remove the thick and fibrous outer layer of each stem.
2. Steam artichokes for 40 to 45 minutes using a steamer basket. (A pot filled with 1 inch of water also may be used. Add artichokes, bring to a low simmer, and keep covered. More water may be needed if evaporation occurs.)
3. Allow artichokes to completely cool before using a sharp knife to trim tops and cut in half lengthwise. Steam longer if artichokes are not easy to cut. Using a spoon, remove the feathery choke (which sits inside at the base of the artichoke) by scraping it away from the heart. Repeat for all artichoke halves.
4. Brush artichokes with olive oil on all sides. On a hot grill or cast iron skillet, grill both sides of each artichoke and the lemon half to create grill marks. Serve with Lemon Aioli (recipe follows).

LEMON AIOLI

Yield: ¾ cup

INGREDIENTS

⅔ cup mayonnaise

1 teaspoon minced garlic

½ teaspoon lemon zest

dash cayenne pepper

½ teaspoon dried chives

1 teaspoon dried oregano

1 teaspoon dried tarragon

1 teaspoon minced fresh chives

2 teaspoons lemon juice

1 tablespoon capers, roughly chopped

DIRECTIONS

Combine mayonnaise, garlic, lemon zest, and cayenne in a small bowl using a whisk or electric mixer until well combined. Fold in remaining ingredients. Keep chilled.

PACIFIC DIP—*PACIFIC TABLE*

Yield: 2 cups

A taste of the Pacific Northwest can be found in Fort Worth at chef Felipe Armenta's Pacific Table, popular for sushi, seafood, steaks, and cocktails. This crowd-pleasing appetizer is easy to whip up and impress guests, whether served with cut vegetables and pita chips or with grilled bread and sliced avocado like at the restaurant.

INGREDIENTS

4 ounces cream cheese

1 ½ teaspoons fresh squeezed lemon juice

2 tablespoons sour cream

3 tablespoons mayonnaise

1 teaspoon horseradish

½ teaspoon Tabasco sauce

6 to 8 ounces smoked trout or salmon, ½-inch diced (Pacific Table uses smoked trout, but smoked salmon is a suitable substitute.)

1 egg, medium boiled, pressed through a fine strainer

4 to 5 green onions, very finely chopped

DIRECTIONS

In a bowl, combine cream cheese, lemon juice, sour cream, mayonnaise, horseradish, and Tabasco with a spatula until smooth. An immersion blender may be used for a more restaurant-style presentation. Gently fold in remaining ingredients.

CHICKEN FRIED TEXAS OYSTERS WITH CHIPOTLE BUTTER & MANGO PICO—*97 WEST KITCHEN & BAR, HOTEL DROVER*

Makes 4 servings

To "chicken fry" means to batter in a combination of seasoned flour and an egg-milk wash. "Chicken-fried," however, can refer to many things in Fort Worth: steak, chicken, and in the case of this upscale Texas-inspired restaurant inside the western chic Hotel Drover, Texas Gulf Coast oysters.

INGREDIENTS

1 cup flour

¼ teaspoon cayenne pepper

¼ teaspoon garlic powder

salt and pepper, as needed

½ cup milk

¼ cup buttermilk

1 egg

oil, as needed for frying, such as canola or vegetable oil

12 Gulf Coast oysters, shucked (or 8-ounce container pre-shucked oysters, drained)

Mango Pico (recipe follows)

Chipotle Butter (recipe follows)

Cumin Crema (recipe follows)

DIRECTIONS

1. Combine flour with cayenne pepper, garlic powder, and a pinch of salt and pepper in a shallow pan.
2. In a separate shallow pan, whisk together milk, buttermilk, and egg.
3. Heat oil to 350 degrees in a cast iron skillet.
4. Dredge oysters in flour to coat on all sides. Transfer oysters to egg mixture and coat completely. Transfer back to seasoned flour to coat on all sides with flour again.
5. Gently place oysters in cast iron skillet and fry for approximately 2 minutes, turning with tongs. Remove from pan and transfer to a paper towel-lined plate briefly before tossing with melted Chipotle Butter while still warm. Place oysters on a serving dish and top each with a bit of Mango Pico and a dollop of the Cumin Crema.

CHIPOTLE BUTTER

INGREDIENTS

4 tablespoons melted butter

1 tablespoon chipotles in adobo sauce

DIRECTIONS

Combine ingredients just before serving.

MANGO PICO

INGREDIENTS

1 mango, peeled and micro diced

½ Fresno chile, seeds removed and micro diced

½ teaspoon red onion, micro diced

pinch salt

DIRECTIONS

Combine all ingredients. Note that the recipe will yield more than needed for garnishing oysters and is great for serving with tortilla or plantain chips.

CUMIN CREMA

INGREDIENTS

¼ cup sour cream

½ teaspoon ground cumin

1 teaspoon lemon juice

pinch salt

DIRECTIONS

Combine all ingredients and keep chilled.

CRAB CAKES WITH REMOULADE SAUCE OVER ARUGULA SALAD WITH CHAMPAGNE VINAIGRETTE—*WINSLOW'S WINE CAFÉ*

Makes 3 servings

While crab cakes originated in the Mid-Atlantic region of Chesapeake Bay, it's possible to find them in non-coastal Fort Worth. This version comes from one of west Fort Worth's favorite neighborhood restaurants, Winslow's Wine Café, and offers some Southern flair with the addition of roasted corn, bell peppers, and remoulade sauce.

INGREDIENTS

1 pound lump crab meat

⅓ cup roasted corn kernels

⅓ cup diced bell pepper (yellow and red preferred)

⅓ cup diced red onion

½ cup breadcrumbs

¼ cup mayonnaise

2 tablespoons Dijon mustard

2 tablespoons olive oil

DIRECTIONS

1. Combine all ingredients in a mixing bowl and form mixture into 6 crab cakes.
2. Heat oil in a large skillet over medium-high heat. Cook the crab cakes until golden brown on both sides, about 5 to 6 minutes total, flipping once. Keep warm.

TO SERVE

To serve this dish as Winslow's does, toss champagne vinaigrette with arugula, diced avocado, and halved cherry tomatoes, to taste, and divide among plates. Sprinkle a little Parmesan Reggiano atop each salad. Serve salad with 2 crab cakes and a small side of remoulade sauce.

REMOULADE SAUCE

Yield: 1 ¾ cups

INGREDIENTS

1 ¾ cups mayonnaise

1 ½ tablespoons capers, chopped

¼ red onion, minced

zest and juice from ½ lemon

1 tablespoon smoked paprika

DIRECTIONS

Combine all ingredients in a small bowl and keep chilled.

CHAMPAGNE VINAIGRETTE

Yield: about 1 ½ cups

INGREDIENTS

1 cup olive oil

½ cup champagne vinegar

¼ teaspoon salt

¼ teaspoon black pepper

DIRECTIONS

Whisk together ingredients to combine.

TEXAS SHRIMP & GRITS—*BONNELL'S FINE TEXAS CUISINE*

Makes 4 servings

Coastal cuisine in landlocked Fort Worth isn't hard to come by thanks to chef Jon Bonnell. The tenured restaurateur's resume includes time in New Orleans, making him a local expert on upscale Southern-inspired seafood. It's the Texas Gulf Coast shrimp and locally sourced grits that makes this recipe authentically Texan, he says.

INGREDIENTS

½ medium onion, chopped

1 teaspoon minced garlic

1 teaspoon butter

2 teaspoons Frank's RedHot® sauce, divided

1 ½ cups heavy cream, divided

1 cup chicken stock, plus more as needed

1 to 2 tablespoons Creole seasoning

½ cup stone ground grits (Waco-based Homestead Gristmill brand is recommended.)

1 ¼ cups grated Monterey Jack cheese

2 links hot Andouille sausage, diced into small cubes

12 to 14 large Texas Gulf Coast shrimp (16-20 count), peeled and deveined

salt and pepper, to taste

chopped parsley and/or thinly sliced roasted pepper, for garnish (optional)

DIRECTIONS

1. In a large pan or pot, sauté the onions and garlic in butter until soft. Add 1 teaspoon hot sauce, 1 cup heavy cream, and the chicken stock and bring to simmer. Be careful not to let the liquids boil over.
2. Quickly whisk in seasoning and grits while simmering. Stir constantly until grits begin to thicken, about 15 to 20 minutes. Add more broth as needed if grits become too thick. Turn heat to low. Gently fold in cheese and let sit for at least 5 minutes.
3. In a separate pan, sauté sausage until slightly browned. Drain off all extra grease.
4. Add the shrimp to the sausage and cook over medium heat for 1 minute. Add remaining ½ cup cream and 1 teaspoon hot sauce and simmer until thickened. Season with salt and pepper as desired, then pour the entire pan over the grits. To serve, garnish with parsley or sliced roasted peppers, or both.

GARLIC-STUFFED BEEF TENDERLOIN WITH WESTERN PLAID HASH AND SYRAH DEMI-GLACE —*LONESOME DOVE WESTERN BISTRO*

Makes 4 servings

This recipe from Tim Love, a chef known for inventive dishes like kangaroo carpaccio and rabbit-rattlesnake sausage, requires some dedication—the veal stock alone will take a day to make. But the attention to detail will result in a home version of one of the finest dishes in Fort Worth.

INGREDIENTS

4 (8-ounce) beef tenderloin fillets

4 garlic cloves, roasted (see note), plus more for the Western Plaid Hash

kosher salt and cracked black pepper, as needed

¼ cup olive oil

Syrah Demi-Glace (recipe follows)

Western Plaid Hash (recipe follows)

DIRECTIONS

1. Heat oven to 350 degrees.
2. Make a small slit in the side of each tenderloin with a paring knife and stuff 1 large clove of garlic in each. Season fillets liberally with salt and pepper on both sides.
3. In a hot sauté pan, add ¼ cup olive oil. Place all 4 steaks in the pan and sear on high for 1 ½ minutes on each side. Place in oven for 4 minutes to achieve medium-rare to medium.
4. To serve, place Western Plaid Hash potatoes in center of plate and top with cabbage and peppers. Place tenderloin on top of cabbage and peppers, then pour Syrah Demi-Glace on top of steak. If desired, garnish with a seasonal green vegetable like grilled asparagus or green beans.

ROAST THE GARLIC

Place fresh, unpeeled cloves in a cast iron skillet or a heavy bottomed sauté pan and roast over low heat for 20 to 30 minutes. Shake the pan occasionally to prevent the garlic from burning or roasting unevenly. Garlic also may be roasted in a 350-degree oven for 20 to 25 minutes until lightly browned. The garlic cloves should be creamy, sweet, and soft enough to squeeze out of the clove skin. Garlic also may be roasted in advance.

SYRAH DEMI-GLACE

INGREDIENTS

½ cup Australian Syrah (plus more for the Western Plaid Hash)

2 cups Veal Stock, reduced by half (recipe follows)

DIRECTIONS

Add wine to a sauce pot and bring to a boil. After half of the wine has evaporated, add Veal Stock and reduce by two-thirds. Keep warm.

WESTERN PLAID HASH

INGREDIENTS

2 cups peanut oil or preferred cooking oil

2 Russett potatoes, peeled, sliced very thin, rinsed in cool water, then patted dry

kosher salt and cracked black pepper, as needed

¼ cup olive oil

1 red bell pepper, sliced very thin

1 cup green cabbage, sliced very thin

1 cup red cabbage, sliced very thin

1 red onion, peeled and sliced very thin

6 garlic cloves, roasted

2 jalapeños, seeds removed and finely chopped

½ cup Australian Syrah

DIRECTIONS

1. Add peanut oil to a 4-quart saucepan or deep fryer and heat to 325 degrees. Carefully drop potatoes in oil, stirring frequently. Cook for approximately 4 minutes, or until golden brown. Remove potatoes from oil and place in a bowl. Season with salt and pepper and reserve.
2. In a large cast iron skillet or flat grill, heat ¼ cup olive oil. Add peppers, cabbage, onions, garlic cloves, and jalapeno. Cook until cabbage is wilted, adding salt and pepper to taste. Add wine to cabbage mixture and simmer until wine reduces. Reserve and keep warm.

VEAL STOCK

Yield: 2 quarts

INGREDIENTS

8 pounds veal bones (or veal and beef bones), cut into 2-inch chunks (visit a local butcher, such as Central Market)

2 medium onions, peeled and coarsely chopped

2 medium carrots, coarsely chopped

1 celery stalk, coarsely chopped

1 leek, coarsely chopped

2 large tomatoes, quartered, or ½ cup tomato paste

1 teaspoon whole peppercorns

2 bay leaves

2 sprigs fresh thyme

8 garlic cloves, smashed

DIRECTIONS

1. Heat oven to 450 degrees.
2. Arrange bones in a roasting pan large enough to create a single layer. Roast until dark golden brown, about an hour, turning occasionally to brown all sides.
3. After 1 hour, add the remaining ingredients to the pan and roast for 30 more minutes. Transfer the bones and vegetables to a large 10- or 12-quart stockpot.
4. Pour off fat from the roasting pan, then deglaze the pan with 2 cups water, scraping up any particles that stick to the bottom of the pan. Pour deglazed mixture into the stockpot with enough additional water to cover the ingredients by 3 inches.
5. Bring the water to a boil, then reduce the heat and simmer uncovered 4 to 6 hours, skimming the foam as it accumulates on top and adding water as needed to keep the bones and vegetables covered at all times.
6. Strain the liquid into a clean pot, pressing to extract all the juices.
7. Reduce stock over medium heat until 2 quarts remain.
8. Cool and refrigerate in a covered container up to 3 days, discarding any hardened layer of fat before using or freezing.

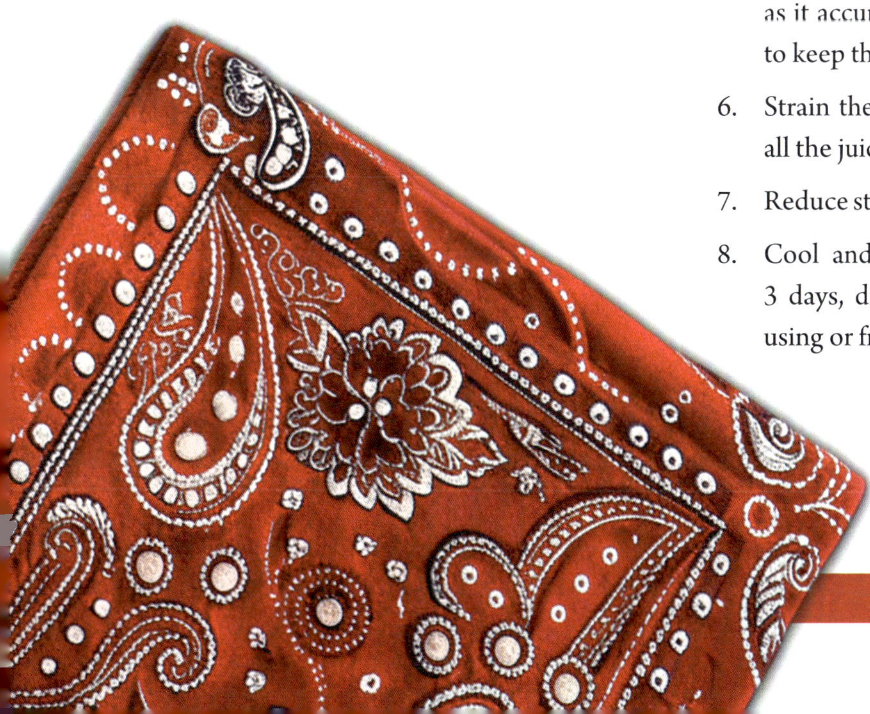

GRILLED RIBEYE STEAK—*THE MEAT BOARD*

Makes 4 servings

Home to real-life ranchers and cattle raisers, Cowtown is known as a steak-lover's oasis. While there's no shortage of steakhouses, a great ribeye (Fort Worth's most popular cut) can be grilled at home thanks to tips provided by The Meat Board butcher shop. This two-step method allows for a crusty char while maintaining a medium rare temperature.

INGREDIENTS

1 ribeye steak, at least 1-inch thick, at room temperature

avocado oil or beef tallow, for searing, as needed

A word on choosing the best ribeye steak: Look for the ribeye cap (or spinalis), a muscle at the top of the steak. The experts at The Meat Board recommend a large, long cap, as it's touted as the most flavorful part of a ribeye.

DIRECTIONS

1. On a very hot grill (at least 450 degrees), grill steak for 2 to 3 minutes per side, just below medium rare.
2. In a cast iron skillet, heat avocado oil or beef tallow. Remove steak from grill and place into skillet to create a good sear on both sides, about 2 minutes per side. Steak may be flipped more than once for extra crustiness, but do not overcook.
3. Let steak rest at least 5 minutes before slicing.

Note:

Seasoning of choice, such as salt, pepper, garlic powder, or steak rub, may be used to season steak before grilling if desired.

Cousins Bar-B-Que

BURGERS & BARBECUE

No need to ask, "Where's the beef?" in Fort Worth. The answer is "everywhere." Burger and barbecue joints abound in Cowtown, from divey destinations that have drawn locals for decades to newer places with more "gourmet" options.

A bit of education on Texas barbecue: there are a few key differences from other barbecue styles. Perhaps the most notable is the traditional cooking method of smoking meats over low temperatures for very long periods, a process dubbed as "low and slow." Second, Texas barbecue is not typically doused in a sauce when served—most places leave that up to the customer. Here, the meat's flavor is the primary focus of a proud pitmaster. Lastly, brisket is considered the signature dish of Texas barbecue . . . and the hardest to prepare.

The family-owned Cousins Bar-B-Q, named as a top 50 barbecue destination in the state of Texas, shares their detailed method for smoking brisket in this chapter, including picking the wood, choosing the beef, trimming and seasoning, starting and maintaining the smoker, and finally slicing the final product.

This chapter also includes methods for barbecue beef ribs by the historic Riscky's Barbecue, open in Cowtown since 1927; perfectly basted backyard barbecue chicken from Michaels Cuisine; and one of Cowtown's most popular eats—the nationally acclaimed bacon burnt ends from Heim Barbecue, which is credited with creating the sweet-and-savory pork belly delicacy right here in Fort Worth.

As for burgers, one of Fort Worth's most beloved burger joints is Fred's Texas Café. The institution is known for its authentic "cowboy cooking," which encompasses dishes like grilled quail, chicken fried steak, and Tex-Mex favorites. Co-owner Quincy Wallace shares his straightforward approach for cooking a great burger, including the all-important "build" that follows.

THE ORIGINAL FREDBURGER—*FRED'S TEXAS CAFÉ*

Makes 4 servings

A tradition since 1978, Fred's sets the standard for two-fisted burgers in Fort Worth. This recipe offers a variation for Fred's Diablo Burger, Fort Worth's first "gourmet" burger that opened the doorway for other nontraditional burgers to follow. Its chipotle peppers are a popular local spice, introduced to many palettes by Fred's chuckwagon-inspired cuisine.

INGREDIENTS

2 pounds 80/20 ground chuck

fresh ground cracked black pepper and coarse kosher salt, to taste

8 slices American cheese

4 hamburger buns (Texas-based Mrs Baird's Bread is recommended)

yellow mustard, as needed (French's® Classic Yellow Mustard is recommended.)

1 small yellow onion, diced

thick-sliced hamburger pickles (Fort Worth–based Best Maid Pickles are recommended), about 5 slices per burger

half-head iceberg lettuce, roughly chopped

2 tomatoes (beefsteak is recommended), cut into 8 ¼-inch slices

DIRECTIONS

1. Heat a cast iron skillet over very high heat. The hotter, the better.
2. Portion beef into 4 equal balls, then carefully form into ¾-inch patties, being careful to not overwork the beef. Season patties with salt and pepper on both sides.
3. Sear patties to medium temperature, approximately 7 minutes total, flipping halfway through. (Note: If patties are not room temperature, they will take longer to cook.) Once flipped, top each patty with 2 slices of cheese.
4. Remove patties and add buns to the skillet, face down, to lightly toast in hamburger grease.

BUILDING THE BURGERS

Add mustard to the bottom bun, followed by diced onions, pickles, chopped lettuce, 2 tomato slices, the patty, then the top bun. Note that the order of the burger build is intentional, allowing the tomatoes to serve as a barrier to the hot patty. The tomatoes will soften as they "cook" while keeping the cold items crisp.

FOR FRED'S DIABLO BURGER

Simply omit the lettuce, tomatoes, and pickles and swap Swiss cheese for the American cheese. Sauté the onions with a small can of chipotle peppers in Adobo sauce (San Marcos brand is recommended) until onions are clear, then deglaze pan with a few splashes of Shiner Bock beer. Add chipotle onion mixture atop Swiss-topped patty.

Photo courtesy of Visit Fort Worth

BACON BURNT ENDS—*HEIM BARBECUE*

Serves 8-10 as an appetizer

The Texas barbecue industry changed forever when Fort Worth native Travis Heim debuted his bacon burnt ends with his wife Emma at a dinner party in 2013. The couple is credited with creating the sweet and spicy morsels of smoked pork belly cubes, and pitmasters across the country have since followed with countless copycat versions.

INGREDIENTS

3 ½ teaspoons Kosher salt

2 tablespoons brown sugar

3-pound slab pork belly, raw and skin-off

Heim Barbecue Burnt End Rub, as needed (available at Heim locations and online at heimbbq.com)

DIRECTIONS

1. Combine salt and brown sugar in a bowl. Rub the pork belly thoroughly with the mixture and place into a large Ziploc® bag or airtight container. Let it rest in the fridge for 3 to 4 days to cure, flipping the bag once a day.
2. Remove the belly from the bag and rinse thoroughly.
3. Heat a smoker to 200 degrees (post oak wood is recommended) and smoke the belly until it reaches an internal temperature of 180 degrees, about 3 hours.
4. Remove meat from smoker and rest on a cutting block until cool. Cut belly into ¾-inch cubes and place into a disposable aluminum foil pan. Season very liberally with rub, covering all sides of chunks for good caramelization.
5. Return pan to smoker and smoke at a higher temperature of 250 degrees for about 2 hours, until the pork belly chunks begin to crisp on the outside. Chunks should be caramelized and super soft, but toothsome. Allow to cool in their own fat before serving.

SMOKED BRISKET—*COUSINS BAR-B-Q*

Serves 15-18

Texas' culinary prowess might lie in the quintessential smoked brisket. Cooked low and slow over wood-burning coals for hours on end, the complicated cut of beef can make or break a pitmaster, whether a backyard novice or a seasoned veteran. Jeff Payne of Fort Worth's time-honored Cousins Bar-B-Q shares his national award-winning method here.

INGREDIENTS

hand-picked wood of choice (Cousins uses green hickory), approximately 14 to 16 medium logs

large sheet of butcher paper

1 (12- to 14-pound) prime brisket

seasoning of choice, such as salt, pepper, and garlic powder, or a 16-ounce bottle of Cousins

BBQ Beef Seasoning (found at Cousins Bar-B-Q and online)

A word about types of brisket. . . . *"There are several grades of brisket out there, from 'select' up to Wagyu," says Payne. "What we are mainly talking about is the amount of fat that runs through the meat. Please don't let the word 'fat' scare you. Fat means many great things when cooking a brisket: it's going to help add forgiveness in the cooking process, it's going to help keep your meat moist, and it's going to help create great flavor."*

STARTING THE SMOKER

1. Place 6 logs in smoker firebox with the smallest logs on bottom, gradually stacking bigger logs toward the top. Allow space for airflow for an easier start.
2. Twist large sheet of butcher paper into a tight rope and slide between the small logs at the bottom. Light paper with a lighter. Once the fire is going, plan to maintain it at 225 degrees throughout the cooking process by adding more wood as needed, about 1 log per hour. The process will take 8 to 9 hours at minimum for a 12- to 14-pound brisket.

TRIMMING & SEASONING THE BRISKET

1. Lay the brisket fat side down onto a cutting board and carve out the sternum. The sternum is a hard chunk of fat that will not break down in the cooking process. Next, before flipping back over, remove any extra fat that would potentially affect the bark in the smoking process. The bark is a flavorful, crispy, dark crust that forms on the outside of the brisket during the slow-smoking process.
2. Flip brisket back over to fat side up. Trim the layer of fat down to ¼-inch thick. Payne says anything thicker won't render well in the cooking process and will provide for too large a fat-to-meat ratio.
3. Next, shave down the "mohawk," or the top point of the brisket, by using a knife to create a more aerodynamic shape with less sharp edges. Don't remove the entire mohawk. Make sure the flattest part of the brisket is at least ½-inch thick. Anything thinner will dry out in the smoking process, says Payne.
4. Once the brisket is completely trimmed, rub it down with desired seasoning on all sides. Do not leave an inch uncovered.

SMOKING THE BRISKET

1. Place the brisket in the smoker, fat side up. Close the lid.
2. Maintain the fire through the smoking process, adding 1 log about every hour until brisket reaches an internal temperature of 203 degrees. (See note.)
3. Pull brisket out of the smoker and set it aside to rest until internal temperature lowers to 150 degrees. Slice and serve.

Note:

Seasoned pitmasters know when smoking a brisket, it will reach what's called "the stall," or a point when the internal temperature will stay between 150 to 170 degrees for several hours. When this occurs, remove brisket from the smoker and wrap tightly in butcher paper. Return brisket to smoker and increase fire temperature to 250 degrees. "This is going to help render your fat and make it melt like butter," says Payne. From this point, the brisket may need an hour or 2 more to reach the final internal temperature of 203 degrees.

BACKYARD BARBECUE CHICKEN—*MICHAELS CUISINE*

Makes 6-8 servings

Charcoal is preferred for this recipe to achieve that ideal "backyard" barbecue flavor. Chef Michael Thomson, a trailblazer in contemporary ranch-style cuisine in Fort Worth, recommends letting the coals burn until they're covered in gray ashes before grilling. Serve this dish with sliced white onions, pickled jalapenos, and fresh rolls, along with a few handwipes.

INGREDIENTS

2 whole chickens, about 3 to 5 pounds each, or 2 packages of prefabricated chickens, including breasts, wings, thighs, and legs

1 gallon Michaels Cuisine Barbecue Chicken Brine (recipe follows)

Michaels Cuisine Roc-Doc-Rub, as needed (available at Michaels Cuisine) or barbecue rub of choice

4 cups Michaels Cuisine Chipotle Barbecue Sauce (available at Michaels Cuisine) or barbecue sauce of choice

DIRECTIONS

1. If fabricating whole chickens, cut each chicken into 8 pieces, including breasts, wings, thighs and legs (2 of each).
2. Place chicken pieces into brine in an airtight container or Ziploc® bags. Brine in refrigerator overnight.
3. Remove chicken from brine and allow to air dry, then season generously with rub.
4. Heat grill to between 325 and 375 degrees. Oil the grates and place chicken pieces on the grill. Allow chicken to charbroil on all sides, turning frequently. When internal temperature reaches 130 degrees, begin basting with barbecue sauce. Allow sauce to dry before applying next coat. Chicken pieces should be coated at least 3 times on all sides. Once fully coated, move chicken to a place of indirect heat on the grill and close lid. Chicken is ready when internal temperature reaches 165 degrees.

BARBECUE CHICKEN BRINE

Yield: 1 gallon (enough for 10 pounds of chicken)

INGREDIENTS

1 gallon (4 quarts) ice-cold water

¼ cup kosher salt

¼ cup granulated sugar

1 tablespoon chipotle chile powder

1 tablespoon poultry seasoning

1 tablespoon garlic powder

1 tablespoon onion powder

1 tablespoon Doc-of-the-Bay seasoning (available at Michaels Cuisine) or seasoning of choice

2 tablespoons freshly ground black pepper

DIRECTIONS

1. Bring 1 quart of the cold water to a boil with salt, sugar, and all seasonings. Boil until salt and sugar are fully dissolved.
2. Add boiled water to remaining ice-cold water. Chill brine to 40 degrees before adding chicken, making sure all pieces are fully covered.

BARBECUE BEEF RIBS—*RISCKY'S BARBECUE*

Makes 2 servings

With styles ranging from smoky to sticky sweet, barbecue ribs are as varied as the regions they're from. In Texas, slow-smoked beef ribs—tender enough to fall off the bone—are most prevalent. Riscky's Barbecue, opened in 1927 by Polish immigrants and now under its fourth generation of ownership, shares a home version of them here.

INGREDIENTS

1 beef rib slab, prime grade (about 6 to 7 ribs per slab)

Riscky's Rub (recipe follows)

DIRECTIONS

1. Dust the top and bottom of rib slab with rub.
2. Smoke at 225 to 250 degrees for 3 to 4 hours until fork-tender. (Riscky's recommends using post oak wood.) Ribs also may be baked in the oven at the same temperature for the same amount of time.
3. Remove from heat and let rest for 30 minutes before slicing and serving.

Note:

This same method may also be used to smoke turkey legs, popular at Fort Worth outdoor events and festivals, especially the Fort Worth Stock Show & Rodeo. A 2-pound turkey leg should be smoked for about 2 hours, or until the internal temperature reaches 165 degrees.

RISCKY'S RUB

Yield: About 1 ½ cups

INGREDIENTS

3 tablespoons chili powder

3 tablespoons paprika

1 tablespoons garlic powder

3 tablespoons coarsely ground black pepper

¾ cup salt

DIRECTIONS

Mix all ingredients until thoroughly combined.

Carne Asada with Cheese Enchiladas, Reata Restaurant
Photo courtesy of Laurie Smith

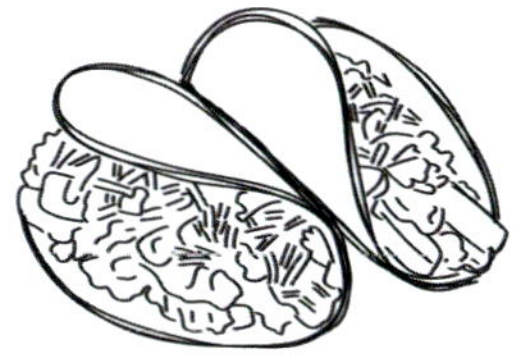

TEX & MEX

Fort Worthians know Tex-Mex is not the same as Mex-Mex, although Tex-Mex is often referred to as "Mexican food." It's enough to make an out-of-towner go "loco."

So, what's the difference?

Historically, many ingredients that were popular during the cattle ranching era weren't used in traditional Mexican cuisine south of the Rio Grande. As the two cultures intermingled throughout the 1800s and into the 20th century, their cooking styles began to influence each other.

Ingredients popular in northern parts of Texas, like ground beef, yellow cheese, and flour tortillas, were used to create Tex-Mex staples like burritos, nachos, and enchiladas. Sour cream was used in place of traditional Mexican crema and shredded cheddar cheese substituted Mexico's crumbly queso fresco. Corn tortillas were cut and fried crispy, paving the way for tortilla chips and salsa to later be named the official state snack of Texas.

Tex-Mex flourished through the 1940s as restaurants continued to fuse flavors from both regions, solidifying the new concept. Several of those Tex-Mex restaurant pioneers came from Fort Worth, including some who share recipes in this book.

Mexican Inn Café opened in 1936 during the height of Tex-Mex cuisine's development. Here they share a recipe for arroz con pollo, which translates to "rice with chicken."

Flour tortillas are made from scratch daily at Mercado Juarez, something that cannot be said by many Tex-Mex restaurants. Find a recipe for making them at home here, and you'll never want to go back to storebought.

Other Tex-Mex staples include fajitas, carne guisada, puffy tacos, green chicken enchiladas, cheese enchiladas, pico de gallo, and guacamole. Recipes for all are listed in this chapter from some of Fort Worth's most respected dining destinations.

Mex-Mex refers to more authentically Mexican menu items, which can be very regional, just like in the US. Dishes like pozole, shrimp ceviche, elote, and tortilla soup are popular in Fort Worth but have much deeper Mexican roots.

FLOUR TORTILLAS—*MERCADO JUAREZ*

Yield: approximately 20 tortillas

There's nothing quite as comforting as a hot, fresh, flour tortilla. Its warmth and softness, whether used as a vessel for tacos or burritos, dipping in queso, or simply slathering with butter, is incomparable to most store-bought varieties from a bag. Mercado Juarez has made theirs from scratch since it opened in 1982.

INGREDIENTS

4 cups all-purpose flour, plus more for work surface

2 teaspoons kosher salt

2 teaspoons baking powder

⅔ cup lard, found in Mexican grocers

1 ¾ cups hot water

DIRECTIONS

1. Whisk together flour, salt and baking powder in a large bowl. Add the lard and incorporate well until mixture is blended and crumbly.
2. Slowly add the hot water and mix with your hands. Knead until dough is smooth and elastic, about 8 to 10 minutes. Knead longer if you prefer lighter tortillas. If dough is sticky to the touch, add ½ teaspoon of flour at a time until it's no longer sticky. Cover with a damp towel and let rest for 20 minutes.
3. Sprinkle flour on kitchen work surface. Grab a golf ball-size amount of dough and roll out with a rolling pin until very thin, one by one. (Size may be larger, if desired.)
4. Heat skillet or comal until very hot and then reduce heat to medium. Add tortillas and heat until they start to bubble around the edges, approximately 30 seconds. Flip and cook for 45 more seconds. Flip one more time and cook an additional 45 seconds. Remove and hold in clean towel or tortilla warmer.

ELOTE—*KOKITOS*

Makes 1 serving

Also referred to as "Mexican street corn," this handheld snack can be found at festivals, local parks, or even parking lots in Hispanic neighborhoods, typically served from a food truck or pushcart. Kokitos opened its first storefront in 2012, making elote easily accessible along with Mexican dessert drinks, fruit cocktails, and more.

INGREDIENTS

2 tablespoons mayonnaise

3 tablespoons sour cream

1 freshly steamed yellow corn on the cob, shucked and skewered for easy holding

3 tablespoons cotija cheese

1 tablespoon melted butter

1 lime

Extra Hot Valentina Salsa Picante, as needed (found at most grocers and Mexican markets)

DIRECTIONS

1. Combine mayonnaise and sour cream in a small bowl and spread mixture on to steamed corn using a spatula or spoon, covering all sides.
2. Cover corn with cotija cheese. Drizzle with melted butter and squeeze juice from lime all over corn. Drizzle with Valentina Salsa and serve.

POZOLE—*TINIE'S*

Makes 6-8 servings

Whether spelled "pozole" or "posole," this brothy pork-based soup is prevalent in Fort Worth Mexican restaurants and Hispanic home kitchens, especially around Christmastime. This red version from Tinie's makes enough to feed a crowd, so invite friends and family over for a hot bowl, holiday season or not.

INGREDIENTS

vegetable oil, as needed

2 ½ pounds pork shoulder, trimmed of excess fat and cut into 4-inch cubes

salt and pepper, as needed

1 large white onion, peeled and roughly chopped

1 ham hock

½ head garlic

5 ancho chiles, stemmed and seeds removed

2 guajillo chiles, stemmed and seeds removed

2 chiles de arbol, stemmed and seeds removed

2 cups yellow hominy, rinsed and dried

2 tablespoons dried Mexican oregano

7 radishes, sliced thin

3 cups green cabbage, sliced thin

DIRECTIONS

1. In a large soup pot, heat a small amount of oil. Season the pork cubes with salt and pepper and brown each side. Add onion, ham hock, and garlic head to the pot. Cover everything with water and bring to a simmer.
2. While the meat is simmering, cover all chiles in warm water and let sit for 20 minutes to rehydrate. Blend chiles with water until smooth using a blender or food processor. Add the chile paste to the simmering pot and cook for 2 hours or until the meat is tender and able to easily pull apart. Skim any excess fat that may rise to the top, as needed.
3. Remove the garlic head and ham hock from the broth and discard the bone, then add the ham hock meat back to the pot. Add the hominy to the pot and simmer an additional 30 minutes. Season with salt and pepper as needed.
4. Serve the pozole topped with dried oregano, sliced radishes, and green cabbage.

Photo courtesy of aye creator

SOPA TARASCA— *DON ARTEMIO MEXICAN HERITAGE*

Makes 6-8 servings

Originating in the Mexican state of Michoacan, this elevated version of traditional tortilla soup comes from the James Beard Award–nominated restaurant Don Artemio Mexican Heritage. Corn tortillas and nixtamal masa, a type of dough made from corn, is blended right into the soup base for rich texture and flavor.

INGREDIENTS

2 tablespoons olive oil

2 garlic cloves, minced

1 medium onion, peeled and chopped

1 dried guajillo chile

2 pounds tomatoes (about 5 to 6), cored and roughly chopped, or a 28-ounce can crushed tomatoes

4 cups water

2 corn tortillas, cut into strips

2 tablespoons nixtamal masa (found in Mexican grocers), or masa harina

salt, to taste

chicken broth, to taste

GARNISHES

diced avocado

panela cheese (found in Mexican grocers), cut into small cubes

lightly fried corn tortilla strips

crushed pork rinds

crumbled cotija cheese

alfalfa sprouts

DIRECTIONS

1. In a deep pot, heat oil and add garlic and onion. Sauté until onions are translucent. Add the chile and sauté briefly.
2. Add the tomatoes, water, tortilla strips, and masa. Bring to a boil, then reduce heat and simmer until the chile softens.
3. Use a high-power blender to blend liquid until smooth. Strain and allow to cool slightly. Adjust seasoning with salt and chicken broth, to taste.
4. To plate restaurant style, arrange garnishes as desired in the center of each bowl, topping with the alfalfa sprouts, then slowly pour in warm soup, about 1 ½ to 2 cups per bowl.

SHRIMP CEVICHE—*TORO TORO*

Makes 4 servings

Shrimp ceviche is a staple in Fort Worth, found on the menu in many Mexican restaurants ranging from corner dives to upscale date-night destinations. This Pan-Latin steakhouse, located inside the iconic Worthington Renaissance Fort Worth Hotel downtown, falls in the latter category. Poached shrimp lends to a quicker prep time.

INGREDIENTS

2 cups shrimp (size 16/20), tails off, peeled, deveined, poached, and chilled

Aguachile Rojo (recipe follows)

fresh ground black pepper and kosher salt, to taste

GARNISHES

1 avocado, diced

1 serrano chile, sliced and seeds removed

2 radishes, thinly sliced

½ red onion, peeled and thinly sliced

1 tablespoon cilantro, chopped

3 tablespoons fresh cotija cheese, crumbled

1 tablespoon crushed pork chicharrónes (pork rinds)

plantain and tortilla chips for serving

DIRECTIONS

1. In a serving bowl, combine the shrimp with the Aguachile Rojo and coat well. Add salt and pepper to taste. Garnish with avocado, serrano chile, radishes, red onion, cilantro, cotija cheese, and crushed pork chicharrónes.
2. Serve bowl over ice with a side of plantain and tortilla chips in a basket.

AGUACHILE ROJO

INGREDIENTS

juice from 4 key limes

4 red Fresno chiles, stems removed

2 habanero peppers, stems removed

2 tablespoons grapeseed oil

kosher salt, to taste

DIRECTIONS

Add all ingredients to a blender. Pulse to desired consistency. Add additional salt to taste.

ARROZ CON POLLO—*MEXICAN INN CAFÉ*

Makes 4 servings

Mexican rice is a staple side dish in Tex-Mex cuisine, typically served alongside refried beans. Its method calls for pan-frying dry rice in oil before simmering with tomatoes, garlic, and spices. At Mexican Inn, which dates back to 1936, it serves as a flavorful base for this comfort food classic.

INGREDIENTS

6 to 8 cups Mexican Rice (recipe follows)

1 ½ pounds shredded chicken (see note)

2 cups Queso (recipe follows)

paprika, for garnish

8 jalapeno slices

DIRECTIONS

Spread 1½ cups Mexican Rice onto each plate. Add about 6 ounces shredded chicken, then top with about a ½ cup of warm Queso. Sprinkle dish with paprika and garnish with 2 jalapeno slices per serving.

Note:

Mexican Inn recommends baking or boiling a whole chicken, shredding by hand to remove all bones, then seasoning as desired. Rotisserie chicken may be used, or any shredded chicken of choice.

MEXICAN RICE

INGREDIENTS

2 to 3 very ripe Roma tomatoes, roughly chopped

½ yellow onion, peeled and roughly chopped

2 garlic cloves, peeled

1 teaspoon chicken base (Knorr is recommended, or 1 cube of any granulated chicken bouillon)

5 tablespoons olive oil

2 cups long grain rice

4 cups water

1 carrot, peeled and diced small

DIRECTIONS

1. In a blender or food processor, add the tomatoes, onion, garlic, and chicken base along with 2 tablespoons of water. Blend to a smooth consistency and set aside.
2. Add the olive oil to a 4-quart saucepan and bring to medium heat, approximately 40 to 60 seconds. Add rice to the warm oil. Be careful not to splash. Stir constantly to ensure the rice fries evenly.
3. Once the rice begins to change color, after about 5 minutes, carefully stir the blended mixture into the pan.
4. Add 4 cups of water to the pan, being careful not to splash. Bring to a boil, then add the diced carrots and stir. Turn heat to low and simmer for 20 minutes, uncovered. Rice should be fluffy and soft when done.

QUESO

INGREDIENTS

1 10-ounce can Ro*Tel® Original Diced Tomatoes and Green Chilis, undrained

1 16-ounce package Velveeta® Original Cheese, cut into ½-inch cubes

DIRECTIONS

Combine the undrained tomatoes and Velveeta into a saucepan. Cook over medium heat for 5 minutes or until Velveeta is completely melted and mixture is blended, stirring frequently. Remove from heat.

GREEN TOMATILLO CHICKEN ENCHILADAS—*ENCHILADAS OLE*

Makes 2-3 servings

"The enchiladas are all about the sauce," says Enchiladas Ole owner Mary Perez, who built a fanbase for her flavorful jarred enchilada sauces before customers encouraged her to open a restaurant in 2013. A hint of curry adds a unique spin on traditional tomatillo sauce. Try Perez's griddle method (instead of the oven) for a restaurant-worthy finish.

Note:

If baking enchiladas is preferred, assemble enchiladas using the same method into a lightly greased glass baking pan and bake at 350 degrees for approximately 20 minutes until cheese is melted and enchiladas are heated through.

INGREDIENTS

10 to 12 tomatillos, husks removed

juice from 1/2 lime

1 teaspoon salt

2 teaspoons curry powder

2 teaspoons garlic powder

6 to 8 corn tortillas

1 pound Grilled Chicken, shredded (recipe follows)

2 cups shredded cheddar cheese

chopped white onions and chopped cilantro, for garnish

DIRECTIONS

1. In a stockpot, add tomatillos and enough water to cover them. Simmer for 20 minutes until soft.
2. Strain tomatillos and add to a blender or food processor with lime juice, salt, curry powder, and garlic powder. Reserve.
3. To prepare enchiladas on a hot stovetop griddle, comal, or even large pan: Dip corn tortillas in water and place on hot griddle. Quickly sear each side, then add approximately 2 tablespoons each of shredded chicken and shredded cheddar cheese in the center of each tortilla. Using a spatula, fold tortillas into thirds, then flip over to create a "seal" on the fold.
4. Pour about ¼ cup to ⅓ cup of reserved tomatillo sauce directly over the top of each enchilada, followed by 2 more tablespoons of shredded cheese. Leave enchiladas on griddle for about 2 minutes, allowing cheese to melt, then top each with a tablespoon each of chopped white onions and chopped cilantro before using a spatula to remove enchiladas from griddle to plates. Serve immediately.

GRILLED CHICKEN

INGREDIENTS

1 pound chicken breasts

chicken rub of choice, as needed

½ cup orange juice

½ cup fresh squeezed lime juice (about 4 limes)

DIRECTIONS

1. Coat chicken thoroughly with rub. Combine with juices in an airtight container or Ziploc® bag and marinate in refrigerator overnight.
2. When ready to grill, bring chicken to room temperature. Grill until chicken is cooked through with an internal temperature of 165 degrees. Allow to cool before shredding by hand or with 2 forks.

PUFFY TACOS—*PULIDO'S KITCHEN & CANTINA*

Makes 4 servings

Resembling crisp, puffed bowls more than actual handheld tacos, these fried corn shells are easy to inhale when stuffed with seasoned ground beef, shredded lettuce, grated cheddar and chopped tomatoes. Pulido's, originally opened in 1966 and reincarnated in 2024, is one of a few establishments that still offer the iconic Tex-Mex dish.

Note:

The experts at Pulido's promise store-bought corn tortillas can puff with a little practice, however homemade corn tortillas might achieve easier results. For homemade corn tortillas, look for masa harina, found at all Mexican grocers and most traditional grocery stores, and follow the package instructions for pressing your own corn tortillas.

INGREDIENTS

1 pound ground beef

2 teaspoons ground cumin

2 teaspoons garlic powder

2 teaspoons chili powder

½ teaspoon salt

8 yellow corn tortillas (see note)

cooking oil, as needed to cover tortillas in a deep fryer or deep skillet

shredded iceberg lettuce, diced tomatoes, and fresh grated cheddar cheese for garnish

DIRECTIONS

1. In a sauté pan over medium-high heat, brown ground beef. Drain off any excess fat and add seasonings and salt. (Note that taco seasoning may be used, if desired.) Set aside and keep warm.
2. In a deep fryer or deep skillet, heat oil to 400 degrees.
3. While the oil is heating, warm corn tortillas in a separate dry skillet or flat top grill. This is an important step for achieving the puffed tortilla.
4. Once oil is heated, place tortillas in fryer, a few at a time depending on space. Do not allow tortillas to touch. Constantly baste tortillas with oil, using a metal spatula or spoon. Once each tortilla puffs up and is golden brown, remove from fryer and place on a paper towel to drain. Let cool for a couple of minutes. This will allow the shells to crisp properly.
5. Carefully poke a hole in the top of the shell and add ground beef, lettuce, tomatoes, and grated cheese to each and serve.

CARNE GUISADA—*ARIZOLA'S MEXICAN RESTAURANT*

Makes 4 servings

Spanish for "beef stew," this comforting dish—studded with tender cubes of beef, softened potatoes, and an array of spices—is a staple menu item in many authentic Mexican food restaurants, as well as home kitchens. Trust this tried-and-true version from the folks at Arizola's, who've been simmering the stew the same way since 1968.

INGREDIENTS

2 tablespoons oil

1 bell pepper, seeds removed and chopped

1 onion, peeled and chopped

2 medium-sized tomatoes, chopped

2 jalapenos, chopped (seeds removed for less spice)

1 pound beef chuck or round steak, cubed

2 large Russett potatoes, unpeeled and cubed

2 bay leaves

1 teaspoon garlic powder

½ teaspoon cumin

1 tablespoon granular chicken base, or 1 chicken bouillon cube

½ teaspoon salt

½ teaspoon black pepper

2 cups salsa of choice

2 cups water

¼ to ½ cup all-purpose flour

DIRECTIONS

1. Heat oil in a large saucepan over medium heat. Add bell peppers, onions, tomatoes, and jalapenos and sauté for 5 minutes.
2. Add beef, potatoes, and seasonings and simmer over medium heat for 10 minutes or until beef is cooked through, stirring occasionally.
3. Add salsa and water, stir to combine, and simmer for 40 minutes.
4. Add flour in ¼ cup increments and stir vigorously to achieve desired thickness. (Not all flour may be needed.) Allow to cool slightly and serve.

DON JUAN COCO VON—*LOS VAQUEROS*

Makes 4 servings

Featuring grilled chicken smothered in a mushroom-wine sauce, this unexpected Tex-Mex dish first appeared on the Los Vaqueros menu when original owner Johnny Cisneros Sr. opened the restaurant in the Fort Worth Stockyards in 1983. It's a play on the classic French coq au vin, with "Don Juan" referring to Johnny himself.

INGREDIENTS

- 3 tablespoons butter, divided
- ½ medium white onion, peeled and diced
- 1 small green bell pepper, diced and seeds removed
- ½ celery stalk, diced
- 1 14-ounce can high-quality, whole peeled tomatoes in juice
- ½ teaspoon salt
- pinch Italian seasoning
- 2 garlic cloves, minced
- ½ chicken bouillon cube (or ⅓ teaspoon chicken base)
- 4 medium chicken breasts, boneless and skinless
- 5 ounces cremini mushrooms, sliced
- ¼ cup red wine (burgundy is preferred)

DIRECTIONS

1. First, make the ranchera sauce. Heat 2 tablespoons butter in a large sauté pan over medium heat. Add onion, bell pepper, celery, tomatoes with juice, salt, Italian seasoning, garlic, and chicken bouillon. Reduce heat to medium-low and simmer uncovered for approximately 30 minutes. The vegetables should be soft and the sauce slightly thickened. Remove from heat and set aside.
2. While the ranchera sauce is simmering, grill chicken breasts as desired, whether on an outdoor grill or stovetop grill. Internal temperature should reach 165 degrees. Keep warm until ready to serve.
3. In a separate small sauté pan, heat remaining tablespoon of butter over medium-high heat. Add mushrooms and sauté briefly until they start to darken. Add wine and sauté 2 to 3 more minutes over low heat.
4. Add mushroom mixture to the ranchera sauce mixture. Smother grilled chicken breasts with the sauce and serve. (Optional: Pop plate in a heated oven first for a few seconds to serve hot restaurant-style.)

CARNE ASADA WITH CHEESE ENCHILADAS—*REATA RESTAURANT*

Makes 6 servings

With five recipes in one, this dish from the legendary Reata Restaurant encompasses both Tex-Mex and cowboy cooking, providing for an authentic taste of Cowtown. Components include Fort Worth culinary staples, like cheese enchiladas, grilled skirt steak (the recipe may also be used for fajitas), guacamole, and pico de gallo.

CHEESE ENCHILADAS

Yield: 12 enchiladas

INGREDIENTS

4 cups Ancho Chili Cream (recipe follows)

12 corn tortillas

4 to 5 cups Monterey Jack cheese, shredded

DIRECTIONS

1. Heat oven to 350 degrees.
2. Lightly coat the bottom of a baking dish with about ½ cup of the Ancho Chili Cream.
3. To assemble the enchiladas, pour about 1 tablespoon of Ancho Chili Cream in a straight line right through the middle of each tortilla, one by one. Scatter 2 tablespoons of the shredded cheese on top of the cream sauce. Roll each tortilla tightly (like a small burrito) and nestle the 12 assembled enchiladas side-by-side in the coated baking dish.
4. Pour leftover Ancho Chili Cream (there should be about 1½ cups remaining) over the top of the 12 enchiladas. Sprinkle leftover shredded cheese (there should about ¾ to 1 cup remaining) over the top of the sauce. Cover with aluminum foil, leaving some space on top so the cheese doesn't stick to the foil.
5. Bake for approximately 15 minutes, or until the cheese on top begins to bubble and the edges of the enchiladas turn a little crusty. Let dish rest 5 to 10 minutes before serving.

ANCHO CHILI CREAM

Yield: 4 cups

INGREDIENTS

16 dried ancho chile peppers, seeds removed

6 to 8 cloves fresh garlic, minced

½ yellow onion, diced

1 ½ tablespoons ground cumin

⅓ cup honey

2 cups water

1 Roma tomato, diced

1 cup heavy cream

DIRECTIONS

1. Rinse the peppers under cold running water, making sure all the seeds are removed.
2. Place the peppers, garlic, diced onions, cumin, and honey in a large stock pot. Add water and simmer over medium-high for 30 minutes.
3. Remove pot from heat and add diced tomato. Let mixture cool thoroughly, then pour mixture into a blender or food processor and puree until fairly smooth.
4. Strain liquid through a fine mesh strainer to remove any remaining pulp or seeds. Place strained liquid in a medium-sized saucepan, add the heavy cream, and bring to a rolling boil. Reduce heat to low and simmer for 10 minutes.
5. Remove pan from heat and let mixture cool thoroughly to thicken before assembling enchiladas.

SKIRT STEAK IN CERVEZA SOAK

Yield: 6 steaks

INGREDIENTS

4 pounds skirt steak, trimmed of any white tissue

1 bottle Corona® beer

juice from 2 limes

½ cup canola oil

DIRECTIONS

1. Marinate steak in beer, lime juice and oil for at least 4 hours, preferably overnight.
2. Remove from marinade and grill over high heat about 5 to 6 minutes on each side for medium rare. Cut into 6 equal portions. (May also be sliced for fajitas.)

GUACAMOLE

Yield: 2 cups

INGREDIENTS

2 ripe avocados

½ medium red onion, minced

1 Roma tomato, diced

2 teaspoons lime juice, freshly squeezed

½ bunch cilantro, stems removed and chopped

2 ½ teaspoons kosher salt, or to taste

DIRECTIONS

Cut avocados in half and remove pits. Dice avocado flesh while still in skin. Gently scoop diced flesh into a bowl with a spoon. Add remaining ingredients and mix well. Serve immediately.

PICO DE GALLO

Yield: 1 cup

INGREDIENTS

1 teaspoon kosher salt

2 Roma tomatoes, diced

½ red onion, diced

¼ bunch cilantro, stems removed and roughly chopped

3 jalapeno peppers, seeds removed and diced

5 fresh limes, juiced

DIRECTIONS

Combine all ingredients in a large bowl and toss well. Serve immediately or refrigerate in an airtight container and shake well just before serving.

ASSEMBLY

For each plate, top each steak portion with 2 warm Cheese Enchiladas. Garnish with a dollop of Guacamole and a scoop of Pico de Gallo.

Japanese Tempura,
Japanese Palace

BEYOND BORDERS

As one of the fastest-growing cities in America—rapidly approaching 1 million residents—Fort Worth is becoming more expansive in its culinary offerings. Diners can find international flavors with Spanish, French, Asian, Italian, and Mediterranean influence pretty easily. As Fort Worth's palette grows for more globally inspired gastronomy, restaurants are following suit.

One of Fort Worth's most popular restaurants is a cozy neighborhood eatery called Tokyo Café, today run by a second generation of the Ho family who opened it in a former Pizza Hut in 1997. Items like tok fries—fresh cut potatoes seasoned with Japanese spices and served with chili mayo—and the beef bowl with rice have become staples in Cowtown's comfort food scene. Owners Mary and Jarry Ho share a recipe in this book for their fan-favorite yakisoba—wok-fried noodles tossed with cabbage, carrots, onions and the all-important furikake seasoning.

But one of the first restaurants to introduce Japanese cuisine to Fort Worth was Japanese Palace, opened in 1975 by a prominent restaurateur named Dave Benson. At the time, hibachi-style dining was not available in Fort Worth, and diners were dazzled by the theatrics of their very own tableside chef. In 1989, Benson's daughter Pam added a sushi bar, making it Fort Worth's first. Pam still owns and operates the restaurant today, and it remains unchanged as a tribute to her father and 1970s aesthetics and culture. She shares a recipe for Japanese tempura that is fun for a dinner party at home.

In 2014, prominent Fort Worth chef and caterer Juan Rodriguez invested in a giant stainless steel pan and introduced Fort Worth to authentic Spanish paella, typically made in massive amounts to feed a crowd. An approachable home version of the recipe can be found in this chapter.

JAPANESE TEMPURA—*JAPANESE PALACE*

Makes 8 servings

Open since 1975, Japanese Palace brought a lot of "firsts" to Fort Worth: first hibachi-style restaurant, first sushi bar, and first instances of Japanese tempura. Today the Eastern-inspired eatery, with its authentic koi pond and original bar and décor, stands like a time capsule of 1970s culture, drawing new generations nightly for dinner.

INGREDIENTS

1 ⅔ cups sifted flour, plus more for dredging, as needed

2 egg yolks

1 ⅔ cups ice water

high-heat oil for frying, such as canola or peanut oil

4 cups fresh vegetables of choice, such as green beans, halved mushrooms, sliced yellow onions, and peeled and sliced sweet potatoes

1 pound extra-large shrimp, raw, deveined, tail on, and scored along bottom to lie flat

DIRECTIONS

1. Add flour, egg yolks, and ice water to a medium bowl and mix using a whisk, fork, or chopsticks until just combined. Do not overmix.
2. In a heavy pan or wok, heat about 2 inches of oil to between 330 to 340 degrees.
3. Dredge vegetables lightly in flour, then in batter to completely coat. Deep fry in small batches until lightly blonde in color, about 1 to 2 minutes for green beans, mushrooms, and onions, and about 3 minutes for sweet potatoes. Turn during the frying process to ensure even cooking. Remove to a paper towel–lined cooling rack.
4. For the shrimp, take each by the tail to dust in flour and then batter. Fry for 2 to 3 minutes, turning once during the frying process. Remove to cooling rack.
5. Serve immediately with Dipping Sauce (recipe follows).

DIPPING SAUCE

INGREDIENTS

¾ cup warm water

3 tablespoons soy sauce

2 teaspoons sugar (see note)

4 tablespoons rice vinegar

DIRECTIONS

Add all ingredients to a small saucepot and bring to a boil for 1 to 2 minutes. Allow to cool before serving.

Note:

If a sweeter, thicker sauce is preferred, more sugar may be added to taste.

CHICKEN KARAAGE—*WABI HOUSE*

Makes 4-6 servings

Fort Worth's own izakaya—a Japanese bar that serves drinks and snacks, similar to a pub—exists thanks to Wabi House, where patrons will find authentic Japanese small plates and an array of rich ramen soups. Big on the menu is chicken karaage—fried bite-sized chicken thighs served with spiced watermelon and Japanese mayo.

INGREDIENTS

1 tablespoon sake

¼ cup soy sauce

1 ½ tablespoons sugar

2 tablespoons minced ginger

1 tablespoon minced garlic

1 ½ to 2 pounds chicken thighs, boneless and skinless, fat trimmed, and cut into 1- to 2-inch cubes

oil for frying

½ cup cornstarch

DIRECTIONS

1. Combine sake and soy sauce in a medium bowl. Add sugar and whisk until dissolved. Add ginger and garlic and stir to combine.
2. Add chicken cubes to marinade and toss to coat. Marinate at least 1 hour and up to 24 hours in refrigerator.
3. In a heavy-duty pot, heat oil to 350 degrees.
4. In a large bowl, add cornstarch and then marinated chicken, tossing evenly to coat.
5. Working in batches if necessary, fry chicken for 5 to 7 minutes or until internal temperature reaches 170 degrees. Remove to a cooling rack.
6. Serve with Spiced Watermelon and Spicy Kewpie Mayonnaise (recipes follow).

SPICED WATERMELON

INGREDIENTS

1 small watermelon, cut into 2-inch cubes

1 lime

1 ½ tablespoons Japanese togarashi seasoning (found at Central Market)

1 teaspoon salt

DIRECTIONS

Place watermelon cubes in large mixing bowl. Squeeze fresh lime juice over watermelon, then season with togarashi and salt. Adjust seasoning to taste. Mix well and keep chilled.

SPICY KEWPIE MAYONNAISE

INGREDIENTS

1 (12-ounce) bottle Japanese Kewpie Mayonnaise (found at most grocers)

1 ½ teaspoons chili oil

1 ½ teaspoons Japanese togarashi seasoning

1 ½ teaspoons cayenne

1 ½ teaspoons paprika

DIRECTIONS

Combine all ingredients in a small mixing bowl and whisk to fully incorporate. Keep chilled.

FRESH PASTA WITH BLISTERED SUNGOLD TOMATO SAUCE—*EMILIA'S*

Makes 6 servings

Fort Worth has experienced a recent boom in Italian dining, where house-made pastas and slow-simmered sauces made with fresh herbs and high-quality ingredients shine amid all the steaks, burgers, and barbecue. This dish from Emilia's, located inside the nationally acclaimed Crescent Hotel, is inspired by the flavors of the Mediterranean coast.

BLISTERED SUNGOLD TOMATO SAUCE

INGREDIENTS

1 tablespoon grapeseed oil (or any high heat oil)

2 pints sungold cherry tomatoes (found at Central Market)

4 garlic cloves, crushed

1 shallot, finely minced

1 cup white wine

2 tablespoons butter, chilled

½ cup fresh basil leaves, lightly packed

zest of 1 lemon, plus lemon juice, to taste

salt and cracked black pepper, to taste

DIRECTIONS

1. Heat oven to 400 degrees.
2. Heat a large, oven-safe pan (stainless steel is preferred) over medium heat until hot. Add oil and heat until shimmering. Add the cherry tomatoes, garlic, and shallots to the pan, tossing a few times to coat in oil.
3. Place pan in oven for 15 minutes or until all cherry tomatoes have burst.
4. Carefully remove pan from oven to stovetop. Add white wine to pan, stirring to deglaze. Remove any tomatoes stuck to the pan.
5. Over low heat, simmer to reduce wine by half. Whisk in cold butter until emulsified.
6. Tear basil by hand and fold into the sauce. Add lemon zest, juice, salt, and cracked black pepper to taste.

FRESH PASTA DOUGH

INGREDIENTS

1 ¾ cups all-purpose flour

½ teaspoon salt, plus more for pasta water

6 large egg yolks

1 large egg

1 tablespoon milk

1 ½ teaspoons olive oil

DIRECTIONS

1. In a stand mixer with a dough hook attachment, add flour and salt. (If not using a stand mixer, see note.)
2. In a separate bowl, whisk together yolks, whole egg, milk, and olive oil.
3. Turn on stand mixer to medium speed. Slowly stream egg mixture into flour mixture while mixer is spinning. Mix until incorporated, scraping sides and bottom as needed. Once fully incorporated, keep on medium speed for 10 minutes to knead.
4. Remove dough and form into a ball. Place back into mixing bowl and cover with a dish towel dampened with warm water. Let sit in a warm, dry place for 1 hour.
5. After the dough has rested, remove from bowl and form into desired pasta shape. To make pappardelle if not using a pasta maker or pasta roller attachment, roll out dough with a rolling pin as thin as possible. Once rolled out, dust the top lightly with flour, then roll up loosely before cutting into 1/2-inch segments. Use fingers to separate strands.
6. To cook the pasta, place in a large pot of well-salted boiling water for approximately 3 minutes or until pasta floats to the top.

BŒUF BOURGUIGNON—*PARIS 7TH*

Makes 4 servings

This traditional French dish originated in Burgundy, France, but Fort Worthians don't need to travel overseas for a taste of the real deal. Paris 7th specializes in fine French cuisine in the classic technique, as illustrated in this at-home method here.

INGREDIENTS

2 pounds beef chuck roast or short rib, trimmed and cut into 1-inch cubes

1 medium white onion, diced into 1/2-inch pieces

3 cups dry red wine, divided (burgundy is preferred)

2 teaspoons kosher salt

1 teaspoon ground black pepper

2 tablespoons butter, divided

4 slices thick-cut hickory smoked bacon, cut into ¼-inch strips

2 cloves garlic, minced

2 tablespoons all-purpose flour

2 tablespoons tomato paste

2 cups beef stock

1 pound carrots, peeled and cut into 1/2-inch slices

3 tablespoons herbs de Provence (without lavender)

1 pound cremini mushrooms, sliced

1 pound pearl onions

½ cup chopped parsley for garnish (or may lightly fry a few stems)

DIRECTIONS

1. Marinate beef and onions in two cups of the red wine for 4 to 12 hours. Drain and save the wine. Season mixture with salt and pepper and reserve.
2. Heat oven to 350 degrees.
3. In a Dutch oven or large pot that will fit in oven, sauté bacon with half of the butter until soft. Remove from pot and reserve.
4. In the same pot over medium-high heat, brown marinated beef and diced onions with garlic. Add flour and tomato paste and stir to coat.
5. Deglaze pot with remaining wine and the reserved wine from the marinade. Bring to boil. Add stock, carrots, bacon, and herbs de Provence. Transfer to oven for about an hour, covered.
6. While beef is in oven, add remaining butter to a pan over medium heat and sauté mushrooms and pearl onions until soft. Garnish dish with mushrooms and onions and a sprinkling of chopped parsley.

Photo courtesy of Jeff Amador

SICILIAN STYLE PIZZA—*ZOLI'S PIZZA*

Yield: 9 square slices

Pizza guru Jay Jerrier graced Fort Worth with authentic Neapolitan and Sicilian-style pizzas when he opened Cane Rosso and Zoli's Pizza. High temps are required for both, yet most home ovens only reach 550 degrees. Here he provides a method for making restaurant-style pizza at home. Or simply visit the restaurant and let the pros do the work.

TOMATO SAUCE

INGREDIENTS

1 15-ounce can crushed tomatoes

½ teaspoon sea salt

1 tablespoon extra virgin olive oil

½ teaspoon dried oregano (freshly dried on a homegrown branch is preferred)

DIRECTIONS

Pulse all ingredients in a blender or food processor. Keep sauce thick and chunky.

SPECIAL EQUIPMENT

Found in culinary stores or on Amazon

- stand mixer with dough hook
- baking steel
- 14 x 14–inch Sicilian pizza pan, at least 1-inch high
- kitchen scale that measures grams (optional)

INGREDIENTS

4 cups (500 grams) bread flour (King Arthur brand is recommended)

1 ½ cups (375 grams) cold water

⅛ teaspoon instant yeast (SAF Instant Yeast is recommended, found on Amazon)

2 teaspoons (10 grams) extra virgin olive oil, plus more as needed

2 ½ teaspoons (15 grams) sea salt

Tomato Sauce (recipe follows)

9 slices of part skim mozzarella (from the grocer's deli is recommended)

toppings of choice, such as pepperoni, sausage, vegetables

Pecorino Romano cheese, grated (Locatelli brand is recommended)

DIRECTIONS

To make the dough, allow 1 to 2 days of prep.

1. Add flour, cold water and yeast to the bowl of a stand mixer fitted with a dough hook. Mix on low for about 3 minutes until the dough comes together into a shaggy ball. Let the mixture sit for about 20 minutes to allow the water to be fully absorbed.
2. Add oil and mix on low for another 3 minutes until oil is incorporated.
3. Add the salt and mix on medium for 2 minutes. Let dough rest for 20 minutes.
4. Oil your hands or dip your hands in water to handle dough. The dough will be sticky. Leave it in the mixing bowl. For the next hour, do a series of 3 stretch-and-folds every 20 minutes. To do this, grab a corner of the dough ball and pull it up to the top of the bowl, then fold it back into the main dough ball. Rotate the bowl a quarter turn and repeat until you've made the full circle.
5. After completing the stretch-and-folds, oil your hands and pick up the dough to form a ball. The dough will be sticky and runny, "so just do the best you can," says Jerrier.
6. Cover the dough ball in the mixing bowl with plastic wrap and refrigerate for 24 to 48 hours. (Tip: A disposable shower cap works great in place of plastic wrap.)

DIRECTIONS

On the day of making pizza:

1. Oil Sicilian pizza pan generously with extra virgin olive oil. Dump the dough ball into the center of pan and flatten a tiny bit so it's below the rim. Cover in plastic wrap or shower cap and leave at room temp for approximately 8 hours. The dough ball will eventually spread and fill the pan. If it doesn't, pull the corners to spread it most of the way and let it rest.
2. Once the dough has filled the pan, drizzle the top with olive oil and make dimples into the dough with fingertips.
3. Heat oven to 550 degrees and place the baking steel on middle rack. If using a convection oven, use the convection setting. Place the dough in the oven (without toppings) on top of the baking steel and bake for 6 to 8 minutes. The dough should be lightly brown and pulled away from the sides of the pan.
4. Remove pizza and let cool for about 15 minutes. (See note.)
5. Lay sliced mozzarella across the top in a 3 x 3 grid. Use extra cheese if there are gaps.
6. Using a large spoon, spread sauce on top of cheese slices. Add any additional toppings at this time and a generous dash of Pecorino Romano. Return to oven on the baking steel and bake 10 minutes or until the sauce is bubbly and cheese starts browning.
7. Remove from oven and let cool for a few minutes. The pizza should release from the pan cleanly. Slide pizza out of pan onto a cooling rack for about a minute, then move to a cutting board and add another dose of Pecorino Romano and drizzle of extra virgin olive oil. Add fresh basil, if desired. To serve, cut into 9 square slices.

Note:

The pre-baked dough may be made a day in advance. Once cooled, wrap in plastic wrap and keep in refrigerator. Bring to room temp before baking.

YAKISOBA—*TOKYO CAFÉ*

Makes 2 servings

For many longtime Fort Worthians, comfort food comes in the form of Tokyo Café's yakisoba noodles. Regulars have tucked into hot bowls of the savory wok-fried dish ever since owner Jarry Ho's parents first opened the iconic Japanese restaurant on Camp Bowie Boulevard in 1997.

INGREDIENTS

2 servings packaged dried yakisoba noodles

4 tablespoons vegetable oil

4 ounces protein of choice, cut into bite-size pieces (chicken, beef, pork, shrimp, or tofu)

½ yellow onion, peeled and sliced

1 small carrot, julienned (about ¼ cup)

1 cup cabbage, cut into ribbons

1 cup Yakisoba Sauce (recipe follows)

green onions, chopped, for garnish

furikake seasoning, to taste (found at Central Market)

DIRECTIONS

1. Cook the noodles according to package instructions and set aside.
2. Heat oil in a large nonstick frying pan over high heat. Add protein until cooked through. Push to one side of pan.
3. Add onion, carrots, and cabbage and stir-fry for about 45 seconds or to desired doneness.
4. Add cooked noodles and the Yakisoba Sauce. Toss until well combined and the sauce has been absorbed by the noodles. Remove from heat and transfer to a plate. Garnish with chopped green onions and a sprinkling of furikake seasoning.

YAKISOBA SAUCE

INGREDIENTS

1 cup water

1 ¼ tablespoons Worcestershire sauce

4 tablespoons soy sauce (Ponlai style is preferred.)

⅛ teaspoon white pepper

⅛ teaspoon ginger powder

⅛ teaspoon granulated garlic

½ tablespoon brown sugar, plus more if desired

DIRECTIONS

Mix all the ingredients together in a bowl and set aside. Keep refrigerated and tightly sealed until ready to use.

PAELLA—*MAGDALENA'S*

Makes 2-3 servings

A taste of the Mediterranean coast can be found in Fort Worth at Magdalena's, where outdoor pop-up supper club parties hosted by celeb chef and owner Juan Rodriguez are a hot ticket. Spanish paella is his signature dish, now a staple in Fort Worth foodie circles thanks to his influence.

INGREDIENTS

1 tablespoon olive oil

1 cup diced chicken, thighs or breast

½ large yellow onion, chopped

2 tablespoons minced garlic

1 cup Sofrito (recipe follows)

1 cup bomba rice (also referred to as "Valencia rice")

4 cups chicken stock or broth

6 large shrimp, peeled, cleaned and deveined

10 mussels, cleaned and beards removed

salt and pepper, to taste

1 cup green peas, fresh or frozen

1 tablespoon chopped fresh oregano

1 tablespoon chopped fresh parsley

lemon wedges (optional)

DIRECTIONS

1. Heat olive oil in a paella pan or large pot over high heat. Add chicken and sear. Add onions, garlic, and Sofrito. Sauté for 2 to 3 minutes.
2. Add rice and mix with wooden spoon until well incorporated. Add chicken broth slowly and stir until rice is evenly distributed. Reduce heat to medium and simmer about 5 to 10 minutes until liquid has reduced by about half.
3. Add shrimp and mussels and stir, cooking just until shrimp turns opaque and mussels open. Season with salt and pepper to taste. Stir in peas. At this point, most of the liquid will be gone.
4. Garnish with parsley, oregano, and optional lemon wedges.

SOFRITO

INGREDIENTS

1 ½ tablespoons olive oil

1 medium yellow onion, diced

1 medium red pepper, diced

1 dried ancho chile pepper, reconstituted in water

2 large garlic cloves, sliced

1 14.5-ounce can crushed tomatoes

1 teaspoon sweet paprika, Spanish preferred (found at Central Market in bulk section)

½ cup sherry vinegar

1 tablespoon freshly chopped oregano

1 cup chicken stock or broth

1 pinch dried saffron

salt and pepper, to taste

DIRECTIONS

1. Sauté onions and red pepper in olive oil in a large pan or pot over medium heat. Add ancho chile pepper, garlic, and tomatoes. Simmer for 2 to 3 minutes.
2. Add paprika, sherry vinegar, and oregano. Stir until well incorporated.
3. Add chicken broth or stock and saffron. Simmer for about 15 minutes until liquid reduces by about half.
4. Let cool, then purée with stick blender or regular blender. (Be sure to let Sofrito completely cool before blending.)
5. Once puréed, return mixture to pan or pot over low heat. Simmer for another 20 to 30 minutes, allowing the Sofrito to reduce even more. If the purée is too thick, add a little more chicken broth or stock, as needed. Rodriguez says the flavor of tomatoes and peppers will shine as the Sofrito reduces.

INDIAN FRY BREAD—*HOOKERS GRILL*

Yield: 8 fry breads

When Ruth Hooker and her mother Kathryn, both members of Oklahoma's Choctaw Nation, opened Hooker's Grill in the Fort Worth Stockyards in 2017, they intended to introduce Texans to Oklahoma's fried onion burger. But their authentic Indian Fry Bread—a doughy, delicious base for sweet and savory toppings—became a customer favorite, too.

INGREDIENTS

2 cups all-purpose flour, plus more for work surface

1 teaspoon salt

3 teaspoons baking power

1 cup lukewarm water

oil for frying (or lard)

DIRECTIONS

1. Combine dry ingredients in a large bowl. Add water and gently use hands to form dough.
2. Let rest for 2 hours covered with a cloth, or overnight in the refrigerator covered in plastic wrap.
3. Bring dough to room temperature when ready to fry. Pinch off about a 2- to 3-inch piece and roll out on a floured work surface until it resembles a tortilla, about 7 to 8 inches wide.
4. Heat oil or lard over very high heat in a skillet, about ¼ inch high. Using tongs, fry one side until golden brown, about a minute, then turn to fry other side. Note that more oil or lard may need to be added to skillet during frying process.
5. Drain on paper towels and serve warm.

Note:

To make Hooker's Indian Taco, top fry bread with taco meat, shredded cheese, shredded lettuce, and chopped tomatoes. The fry bread may also be simply served with honey.

Chicken Fried Steak with Country Gravy, H3 Ranch

HOME COOKING
IN COWTOWN

This chapter is where readers will find Cowtown comfort food classics that might provide a feeling of nostalgia: King Ranch casserole, warm chili, and the almighty chicken fried steak with country gravy, all dishes deeply rooted in Texas' culinary history.

According to the Texas Restaurant Association, Texans order 800,000 chicken fried steaks a day. There's even an official Texas Chicken Fried Steak Day, which falls on October 26 as designated by the Texas State Legislature.

The version featured here comes from H3 Ranch, a restaurant in the Fort Worth Stockyards offering several dishes that date back to Cowtown's cattle driving days. Think steaks grilled over hickory wood flames and oatmeal flapjacks during weekend brunch. The "H3" stands for the three Hunter brothers, Robert, William, and David, Scotland natives who found their way to Fort Worth when they established a livestock commission company in 1873 with offices in the Stockyards.

In 1977, chili was adopted as Texas' official state dish, which originated with Tex-Mex influences as chili con carne. Find a local award-winning version in the following pages from The Honky Tonk Kitchen at Billy Bob's Texas, the world's largest honky tonk—or "country dance hall" for out-of-towners.

The chapter continues with recipes for stick-to-your ribs dishes like corn chowder made with a spicy kick of roasted poblano peppers from one of Fort Worth's hottest new hotels, the rustic-luxe Bowie House; deviled eggs made decadent with the addition of Creole shrimp from Lili's Bistro; and classic fried catfish from the time-honored Tommy's Hamburgers. The owner says the lemon pepper seasoned fillets are surprisingly one of the burger joint's most popular menu items.

OKRA FRIES—*JD'S HAMBURGERS*

Makes 4-5 servings

Prevalent in Southern cooking, fried okra is typically found on restaurant menus thickly sliced and coated in cornmeal. Not at JD's Hamburgers, where owner Gigi Howell serves thin and crispy okra "fries" to accompany her mouthwatering burgers—no batter required. The long and skinny slice takes time, she says, but is well worth it.

INGREDIENTS

1 pound okra

1 teaspoon garlic salt

1 teaspoon onion powder

1 teaspoon salt

1 teaspoon pepper

1 teaspoon cayenne pepper (or ½ teaspoon if less spice is preferred)

canola oil for frying

DIRECTIONS

1. Slice okra stalks longways into quarters, leaving seeds intact. (The seeds will become crunchy and add texture.)
2. Combine spices in a large bowl and set aside.
3. Add canola oil to a cast iron skillet, filling about halfway, and bring to high heat. (A deep fryer may also be used.) Fry okra in batches, being careful not to overcrowd the pan, until they begin to turn dark green, approximately 4 to 5 minutes or until desired crispiness.
4. Remove okra from oil and toss in spice mixture, to taste. Serve with desired dipping sauce, although Sriracha aioli is recommended.

CREOLE DEVILED EGGS—*LILI'S BISTRO*

Yield: 2 dozen

There's nothing devilish about these delicious deviled eggs from longtime landmark Lili's Bistro, which touts unpretentious global cuisine. Tinged with Creole mustard and topped with blackened shrimp, the showstopping starter will turn heads at any dinner party.

INGREDIENTS

12 large eggs

¼ cup mayonnaise

2 tablespoons Creole mustard, such as Zatarain's

2 teaspoons blackening seasoning (Chef Paul Prudhomme Blackened Redfish Magic is recommended), plus more for shrimp, as needed

1 tablespoon honey

½ red bell pepper, finely chopped

2 celery stalks, trimmed of leaves and finely chopped

½ medium red onion, minced

24 medium-size shrimp (26-30 size)

bacon bits, for garnish

chopped green onions, for garnish

DIRECTIONS

1. Fill a large pot with just enough water to cover eggs. Cover and bring to a boil. Allow to boil for 28 minutes (set a timer) and let a little steam release while boiling. Remove from heat, drain water, and add ice water to eggs to chill.
2. Once eggs are completely cold, peel and cut in half lengthwise. (Peel under running cold water and shells should almost fall off.) Remove yolks to a large bowl.
3. Add mayonnaise, mustard, blackening seasoning, and honey to yolks and whip together using an electric mixture on medium speed until combined. Fold in red bell pepper, celery, and onion. Use a spoon to dollop yolk mixture into each egg half. (A piping bag also may be used.) Keep chilled.
4. Heavily coat shrimp with blackening seasoning. Sauté or grill until just done and allow to completely cool.
5. To serve, set 1 shrimp in yolk mixture in each egg, all facing the same direction for ideal presentation. Garnish with bacon bits and chopped green onions.

KING RANCH CASSEROLE—*ROY POPE GROCERY*

Makes 6-8 servings

Dating back to the mid-20th century, this Tex-Mex-influenced dish (likely derived from chilaquiles) is named for the legendary King Ranch in Kingsville, Texas. This updated version from the iconic Roy Pope Grocery, open since 1943, uses a butter and flour roux in lieu of canned soup that's prevalent in most home recipes.

INGREDIENTS

5 tablespoons butter, divided

1 medium onion, chopped

1 medium poblano pepper, seeds removed and chopped

1 10-ounce can Ro*Tel® Original Diced Tomatoes and Green Chilis, undrained

2 tablespoons chopped pimientos

3 to 4 cups cooked chicken, diced (preferably a mixture of dark and white meat)

⅓ cup chopped green onions

2 large cloves garlic, minced

½ teaspoon chili powder

3 tablespoons all-purpose flour

¾ cup chicken broth

¾ cup buttermilk

salt and fresh ground pepper, to taste

canola oil, as needed for frying

8 corn tortillas

2 cups grated cheddar cheese

DIRECTIONS

1. For the filling, warm a heavy skillet over medium heat. Add 2 tablespoons of the butter and sauté the chopped onions, chopped poblano pepper, Ro*Tel®, and pimientos until onions are transparent, about 4 to 5 minutes.
2. Fold the diced chicken and green onions into mixture, combining well. Remove from heat and set aside.
3. For the sauce, in a separate skillet over medium-low heat, melt remaining butter. Add the garlic and chili powder and sauté for 1 minute.
4. Raise the heat to medium. Add flour and stir to combine. Pour in a small amount of broth, stirring constantly to remove lumps. Gradually add remaining chicken broth and the buttermilk while continuing to stir until sauce is thickened, about 3 to 4 minutes. Add salt and pepper to taste. Remove from heat and set aside.
5. Heat oven to 350 degrees. Grease a 9 x 13 baking dish.
6. In a small skillet, heat half an inch of canola oil over high heat. Using tongs, dip tortillas into oil for a few seconds to soften, one by one. Reserve.
7. Cover bottom of baking dish with 4 softened tortillas. Layer with half of the chicken mixture, then top with half of the grated cheese and half of the sauce. Repeat layers beginning with remaining tortillas. Bake for 30 minutes until casserole is heated through and bubbly.

Photo courtesy of Lauren Cook

Photo courtesy of Lauren Cook

CHICKEN PESTO MEATBALLS—*MARGIE'S ITALIAN GARDENS*

Makes 2-3 servings

First opened in 1953 by Italian immigrant Margie Walters, this west Fort Worth institution was revitalized in 2025 by new owner Gigi Howell, who grew up in the restaurant thinking Margie was her grandmother. (Her parents met while working there.) This refreshing spin on meatballs is Gigi's ode to Margie, the original "Mama Meatball."

INGREDIENTS

1 pound ground chicken

1 egg

¼ cup finely shredded parmesan cheese

¼ cup pesto sauce (store-bought or premade)

1 cup seasoned panko breadcrumbs

1 tablespoon garlic powder

1 tablespoon onion powder

1 teaspoon dried oregano

1 teaspoon dried basil

½ cup olive oil

DIRECTIONS

1. In a bowl, add ground chicken, egg, parmesan cheese, and pesto and mix by hand until well combined.
2. Add breadcrumbs and remaining seasonings to meat mixture and mix well. Roll by hand into 2-ounce portions, about 8 meatballs total.
3. Heat olive oil in a large sauté pan over medium heat. Sear each meatball in the hot oil until golden brown on all sides and until internal temperature reaches 165 degrees. Remove to a tray or plate lined with paper towels. May be served over linguini tossed with more pesto, or simply on their own.

CARROT GINGER SOUP—*LOCAL FOODS KITCHEN*

Makes 4 servings

Cowtown is not all meat and potatoes, as proven by the popularity of Local Foods Kitchen, a cozy café with grab-and-go meals boasting a chef's case full of scratch-made, vegetable-centric comfort favorites. This healing soup can be made using fresh farmers market ingredients and is perfect for warming the soul.

INGREDIENTS

2 tablespoons olive oil

2 pounds carrots, peeled and roughly chopped

2 medium yellow onions, peeled and roughly chopped

1-inch chunk of fresh ginger, peeled (may use 3 teaspoons minced ginger)

3 cups chicken or vegetable stock

2 tablespoons fresh minced garlic

3 tablespoons honey

2 tablespoons Sriracha

1 medium lime, juiced

½ tablespoon salt

½ tablespoon fresh cracked pepper

1 ½ cups heavy cream (may substitute a 13.5-ounce can unsweetened coconut milk)

DIRECTIONS

1. In a stock pot, heat olive oil and add carrots, onions, and ginger. Sauté over medium heat for 3 to 4 minutes.
2. Add stock to the pot along with garlic. Gently simmer vegetables until tender, about 30 minutes.
3. Once vegetables are tender, use an immersion blender to blend the ingredients in the pot. A conventional blender may be used by carefully ladling in ingredients. Contents will be hot.
4. Once the contents are pureed, add honey, Sriracha, lime juice, salt, and pepper and blend briefly again. (If using a conventional blender, return ingredients to stock pot after blending.) Stir in heavy cream or coconut milk, and adjust thickness with extra stock, if desired. Adjust salt and pepper to taste once all ingredients have been combined.

AWARD-WINNING CHILI—*THE HONKY TONK KITCHEN AT BILLY BOB'S TEXAS*

Makes 8 servings

Country music and chili are both deeply rooted in Texas history. It's only fitting that the world's largest honky tonk would serve an award-winning version of the pleasantly piquant comfort food. In true Texas fashion, this chili boasts no beans. But smoked brisket is featured as a surprise ingredient.

INGREDIENTS

2 pounds ground beef, such as 80/20

1 to 2 tablespoons olive oil

½ yellow onion, diced

4 cloves fresh garlic, minced

2 tablespoons chili powder

2 tablespoons cumin

1 teaspoon cayenne pepper

1 tablespoon plus 1 teaspoon onion powder

1 tablespoon plus 1 teaspoon garlic powder

salt and pepper, to taste

1 tablespoon sugar

1 ½ cups beef stock

1 teaspoon dried oregano

2 tablespoons smoked paprika

1 (14-ounce) can crushed tomatoes

1 poblano pepper, grilled (over an open flame or cast iron skillet) peeled, seeds removed, and chopped

¼ pound lean brisket, chopped (found at any local barbecue joint, including The Honky Tonk Kitchen at Billy Bob's Texas)

DIRECTIONS

1. Brown ground beef in a large stock pot and drain off excess oil. Set aside.
2. In a small pan, heat oil and sauté onions and garlic until onions are transparent. Add onions and garlic to ground beef along with remaining ingredients. Bring to low boil then reduce heat and simmer for 45 minutes, uncovered.
3. Remove from heat, cover, and let rest for 1 hour before reheating to serve.

CORN CHOWDER—
BRICKS & HORSES, BOWIE HOUSE

Makes 3-4 servings

While chowder is most recognized for having seafood components, it can refer to any thick and texture-rich soup, such as potato and chicken, or in this case, corn. But like all of Bricks & Horses' Southern-inspired dishes, this corn chowder is far from basic thanks to homemade stock and an intricate display of garnishes.

INGREDIENTS

4 tablespoons (½ stick) unsalted butter

3 garlic cloves, sliced

½ medium onion, diced

1 poblano pepper, roasted, seeds removed, and diced (reserve about 1 tablespoon for garnish)

kosher salt, to taste

4 corn cobs, kernels sliced (reserve 2 to 3 tablespoons for garnish and cobs for stock)

2 small Yukon gold potatoes, peeled and diced (about ½ cup)

3 to 4 fresh thyme sprigs

1 teaspoon ground turmeric

3 cups whole milk

3 cups Corn Stock (recipe follows)

½ red bell pepper, roasted, seeds removed, and diced

1 lime

sour cream, as needed for garnish

Calabrian chili oil, as needed for garnish (or hot sauce of choice)

¼ bunch cilantro for garnish, stems removed and roughly chopped

tortilla chips, as needed for garnish (or may use crispy fried tortilla strips)

DIRECTIONS

1. In a large stock pot, heat butter and garlic over low heat until butter melts and garlic softens. Add onions, poblano peppers, and salt and lightly sauté for 15 to 20 minutes, stirring every 2 to 4 minutes to avoid any caramelizing. (The salt is important to allow vegetables to "sweat" and not caramelize, which will provide for more depth of flavor while building the soup.)
2. Add corn kernels and another pinch of salt and sauté for 3 to 4 more minutes. Add the potatoes, thyme sprigs, and turmeric, and sauté for 2 to 3 more minutes, continuing to avoid any caramelization.
3. Add milk and Corn Stock to pot. Season with another small pinch of salt. Bring to a boil then reduce to low heat. Simmer, uncovered, until potatoes are fully cooked, about 20 minutes.
4. Remove thyme sprig stems and transfer soup to a blender while the soup is still hot. Blend on high until smooth. Be careful not to fill the blender more than halfway as liquid will expand. Work in batches if necessary. Add soup back to stock pot, straining, if desired, for a smoother consistency. Season with salt to taste and keep warm.
5. Over high heat in a small pan, quickly sauté the reserved corn kernels and roasted diced peppers until corn is cooked through. Season with salt and finish with a squeeze of lime juice.
6. To plate, divide corn and pepper mixture across bowls, placing a small scoop into center of each. Add a dollop of sour cream on top before pouring in soup. Garnish with chili oil (or hot sauce), tortilla chips, and chopped cilantro.

CORN STOCK

INGREDIENTS

4 corn cobs, corn kernels removed

12 cups cold water

DIRECTIONS

Place cobs and cold water into a pot and bring to a boil. Reduce heat and simmer for 20 to 30 minutes until corn flavor has infused into the liquid. Strain liquid and reserve.

FRIED CATFISH—*TOMMY'S HAMBURGERS*

Makes 4 servings

Fundamental to Fort Worth's food culture is the unpretentious golden fried catfish, found on more area restaurant menus than many may realize. Whether served in baskets or plated with sides, the comfort dish harkens memories of a simpler time, perhaps fishing with family as a child. Tommy's cuts their fillets into strips for a crispy finish.

INGREDIENTS

6 to 8 catfish fillets, cut into strips (see note)

lemon pepper seasoning, as needed

1 cup yellow cornmeal, plus more if needed

vegetable oil for frying, as needed

DIRECTIONS

1. Season catfish strips with lemon pepper seasoning.
2. Add cornmeal to a shallow dish. Dredge the seasoned strips and coat evenly.
3. In a large cast-iron skillet or a Dutch oven, pour about 2 inches of oil and heat to 350 degrees. Fry the strips in batches for about 5 minutes, turning once until golden. Drain on paper towels. Serve hot.

Note:

This recipe may be used for additional species of fish, including tilapia, crappie, and white bass—the latter more commonly referred to as "sand bass" in Fort Worth. Catch your own for a dynamite dinner.

CHICKEN FRIED STEAK WITH COUNTRY GRAVY—*H3 RANCH*

Makes 6 servings

The epitome of Southern cooking might be found in the classic chicken fried steak, which some claim originated in Texas in the 1800s. This version from H3 Ranch in the Fort Worth Stockyards, which is doused in peppery country gravy, is as authentic as it gets.

INGREDIENTS

Seasoned Flour, as needed (recipe follows)

Buttermilk Wash, as needed (recipe follows)

4 cups peanut oil

6 (4-ounce) cube steaks, pounded with a meat tenderizer to approximately 4 x 4 inches

Country Gravy (recipe follows)

DIRECTIONS

1. Set up a breading station with 1 pan of Seasoned Flour and 1 pan of Buttermilk Wash. (Reserve 3 tablespoons of the seasoned flour for the Country Gravy.)
2. Heat oil in a cast iron skillet to 350 degrees.
3. Place steaks in seasoned flour and dredge to coat completely on all sides. Press slightly. Transfer to Buttermilk Wash and coat completely. Transfer back to flour to coat on both sides, pressing down on steaks with the heel of hand to create thinner steaks. Continue to press steaks until steaks grow in size and flour begins to adhere to the meat. The steaks should be approximately 7 x 5 inches and thin.
4. Using both hands, lay steaks gently into hot oil. Allow to fry for approximately 2 minutes on one side, then flip over to finish cooking for about 3 or 4 more minutes. Remove from the oil using tongs, and transfer to a paper towel-lined plate.
5. Add to a plate and cover with Country Gravy to serve.

SEASONED FLOUR

INGREDIENTS

2 cups all-purpose flour

½ teaspoon cayenne pepper

1 ¼ teaspoons onion powder

¾ teaspoon garlic powder

1 teaspoon kosher salt

DIRECTIONS

Place all ingredients in a bowl and whisk until completely incorporated.

COUNTRY GRAVY

INGREDIENTS

2 cups whole milk

3 tablespoons unsalted butter

3 tablespoons seasoned flour

½ cube chicken bouillon (or 1/2 teaspoon chicken base)

¼ teaspoon ground white pepper

¼ teaspoon ground black pepper

DIRECTIONS

1. Heat milk in a small sauce pot. Keep warm.
2. In a separate sauce pot, heat butter and stir until melted but not browned. Whisk in flour in small amounts and cook until pasty.
3. Add the warm milk to the flour mixture and whisk until smooth. Add the chicken bouillon and peppers and cook for 15 minutes over medium low heat or until thickened to desired consistency. Serve immediately or keep warm until ready to use.

BUTTERMILK WASH

INGREDIENTS

1 cup buttermilk

1 cube chicken bouillon (or 1 teaspoon chicken base)

¼ teaspoon garlic powder

1 ½ teaspoons paprika

1 ½ teaspoons dry mustard

DIRECTIONS

Place all ingredients in a bowl and whisk until completely incorporated.

BUFFALO WINGS—*BUFFALO BROS*

Makes 3-4 servings

While Buffalo, New York, is 1,400 miles from Fort Worth, great Buffalo wings exist in Cowtown thanks to chef Jon Bonnell, who partnered with Buffalo native Ed McOwen to open Buffalo Bros in 2007. Their key to great wings is buying the top grade to start, never frozen and never the "small guys," Bonnell says.

INGREDIENTS

- 2 dozen Grade A, extra-large, fresh chicken wings (not frozen)
- oil, enough to cover the wings for deep frying (peanut oil is recommended, but canola oil will work)
- 1 (12-ounce) bottle Frank's RedHot® Sauce

DIRECTIONS

1. Rinse wings in cold water, then allow to completely dry before frying.
2. Heat oil to 350 degrees in a deep fryer or large pan. Add wings and fry for approximately 12 minutes until cooked through, shaking fryer basket occasionally. If pan frying, use tongs to keep wings separated. Fry time may vary depending on wing size. Wings should be crispy and golden brown.
3. Drain off any excess oil, then place in a large mixing bowl with plenty of Frank's RedHot® Sauce. Toss the wings until fully coated, then plate immediately and serve hot with celery sticks, carrot sticks, and blue cheese dressing, if desired.

Chilaquiles, Righteous Foods

LET'S BRUNCH

Brunching has become a sport in modern day dining, and Fort Worth is a winner in the category thanks to its long list of brunch spots that span beyond basic breakfast.

Contemporary early morning destinations liked Brewed have elevated Fort Worth's breakfast scene with craft coffee, and even a full bar with coffee cocktails, along with brunch served all day.

But for many Cowtown diners, breakfast doesn't need to be fancy. Hash browns, over- easy eggs, and crispy fried bacon paired with a bottomless pot of coffee are enough to start the day.

Paris Coffee Shop, open since 1926, has long remained a place for just that, drawing regulars over generations for iconic dishes like buttermilk biscuits and gravy.

But Texas can't officially claim the indulgent combination—some say biscuits and gravy were born in southern Appalachia in the late 1800s as a cheap and calorie-heavy meal well-suited for feeding sawmill workers.

Two more quintessential Cowtown brunch-time favorites feature international flavors. One is chilaquiles, a staple in Mexican cuisine made with fried tortilla strips simmered in a brothy sauce, be it red or green, and often served with eggs sunny side up. Like biscuits and gravy, chilaquiles can be found on upscale brunch menus as well as divey hole-in-the-wall breakfast joints, where English is often a second language.

But there's only one place in town for one of Fort Worth's most celebrated breakfast items: German pancakes from Ol' South Pancake House. The 24-hour diner serves the oven-baked dish at any hour, complete with a tableside presentation. Servers bring two folks to spread and fold in freshly squeezed lemon juice and powdered sugar to finish the giant pancake to order. It's a bucket list experience in Cowtown, one that can now be replicated at home using the recipe shown here.

BUTTERMILK BISCUITS & GRAVY—*PARIS COFFEE SHOP*

Yield: 6 biscuits

Open since 1926, Paris Coffee Shop has welcomed generations of Fort Worthians (along with countless celebrities) for diner fare that harkens a simpler time. Amid the popular pies, chicken and dumplings, bacon and eggs, and cinnamon rolls, Paris' classic biscuits and gravy might be the iconic landmark's most sought-after dish.

INGREDIENTS

- 2 cups all-purpose flour
- 6 teaspoons baking powder
- 1 teaspoon kosher salt
- ½ cup grated frozen butter (see note)
- ¾ cup buttermilk
- 2 eggs
- 1 tablespoon water

DIRECTIONS

1. Heat oven to 400 degrees. Line a baking sheet with nonstick parchment paper.
2. In a large bowl mix together flour, baking powder, and salt. Add frozen grated butter to the flour mixture and stir with a fork until combined. The mixture will resemble coarse crumbs.
3. In a separate small bowl, whisk together buttermilk and 1 egg until evenly combined. Fold the wet mixture into the flour mixture with a spatula until the dough just comes together. Be careful not to overwork the dough.
4. Place the dough on a well-floured surface. If the dough is too sticky, add more flour until it becomes manageable. When the dough is cohesive, fold it in half over itself and gently press to flatten. Rotate the dough 90 degrees and fold it in half again. Repeat this process 5 to 6 times being cautious not to overwork the dough.
5. Roll the dough out to about 1 inch thick. Lightly flour a 3-inch round biscuit cutter and press it straight down into the dough to cut out biscuits. Do not twist the cutter when pushing down; doing so will seal the edges of the biscuits, which will affect how high they rise. Place each biscuit onto prepared baking sheet, ¼ inch apart. Gently rework the remaining dough to cut out 1 to 2 more biscuits, ensuring there are at least 6 biscuits.
6. In a small bowl, whisk together remaining egg and 1 tablespoon water to create an egg wash. Brush the top of each biscuit with the egg wash before baking for 15 to 20 minutes, or until the tops are golden brown. Remove from oven and let sit for 10 minutes before serving.

PARIS CREAM GRAVY

INGREDIENTS

4 tablespoons bacon grease

3 tablespoons all-purpose flour

2 cups whole milk

½ teaspoon salt

½ teaspoon coarse black pepper

½ teaspoon garlic powder

¼ teaspoon onion powder

½ dash of Tabasco

DIRECTIONS

1. In a saucepan over medium heat, add bacon grease and heat until liquified. Sprinkle in the flour and whisk until all dry pockets are incorporated with the bacon grease. Let mixture cook for 2 to 4 minutes, whisking constantly.
2. Once the roux starts to puff up and develop a slight blonde color, gradually stir in milk. Add remaining ingredients while continuing to stir. Cook until the texture is creamy and free of lumps.

CHILAQUILES—*RIGHTEOUS FOODS*

Makes 4 servings

Dating back centuries to the Aztecs, this versatile Mexican dish features lightly fried tortillas as a primary ingredient. Chilaquiles may be red or green, depending on the color of salsa used, and is popular in Fort Worth brunch culture. Lanny Lancarte, a descendent of Joe T. Garcia's Mexican restaurant family, shares his authentic method here.

INGREDIENTS

2 tablespoons olive oil

4 stale corn tortillas

Red Salsa (recipe follows)

8 organic eggs

4 tablespoons Mexican crema (found in Mexican grocers)

4 tablespoons queso fresco (found in Mexican grocers)

DIRECTIONS

1. Add olive oil to a very large, deep pan over medium heat until shimmering, but not smoking. If oil starts to smoke, lower heat.
2. Lightly fry all tortillas until no longer bubbling. Add about 1 cup of salsa to tortillas in the pan, being sure to cover all tortillas. Cover with a lid until tortillas are softened as desired.
3. In a nonstick skillet, fry eggs over-medium or to desired doneness.
4. To serve, scoop 2 heaping servings of tortilla mixture onto each plate. Top each with 2 eggs, 1 tablespoon Mexican crema, and 1 tablespoon crumbled queso fresco.

RED SALSA

Yield: 2 cups

INGREDIENTS

2 chiles de arbol, seeds removed and deveined

6 Guajillo chiles, seeds removed and deveined

2 garlic cloves, roasted

1 (14-ounce) can crushed tomatoes

juice from ½ lime

1 tablespoon diced onions, caramelized

⅛ teaspoon ground cumin

salt, to taste

DIRECTIONS

1. Toast chiles in nonstick pans for 10 seconds on each side over medium heat, being careful not to burn. (If chiles start to smoke, they are burning.)
2. Fully submerge toasted chiles in hot water to rehydrate. Keep submerged for 30 minutes.
3. Remove chiles from water and blend with remaining ingredients in a blender. (May use chicken stock or water to adjust consistency of salsa in the blender.) Season with salt to taste.

WORLD-FAMOUS GERMAN PANCAKE—*OL' SOUTH PANCAKE HOUSE*

Makes 1 serving

So world famous, no other restaurant in town dares to replicate them. However, Ol' South Pancake House, the 24-hour home cooking diner open since 1962, is happy to share the recipe for their lemony-sweet, internationally popular fluffy pancake, as long as one purchases the pancake mix from their store.

INGREDIENTS

1 ¾ cups Ol' South Pancake House German Pancake Mix (available at Ol' South Pancake House and online at olsouthpancakehouse.com)

7 eggs

1 ½ cups milk

4 tablespoons butter, melted, plus more for greasing baking pan

powdered sugar, as needed

1 lemon, halved

DIRECTIONS

1. Add pancake mix to a large bowl. Add eggs, milk, and melted butter and whisk or stir vigorously until all ingredients are thoroughly blended. Cover and place in refrigerator overnight.
2. Heat oven to 450 degrees. Coat a round baking pan with butter, then add batter. Bake 5 minutes until pancake is set.
3. Remove pancake to a serving plate. Sprinkle liberally with powdered sugar, then squeeze lemon juice over the top. Using 2 forks (just like in the restaurant), spread the lemon juice all over the pancake, mixing with the powdered sugar. Use forks to fold pancake into thirds, omelet-style, then into thirds once more to create a thick square.

SOUTH
PANCAKE
FORT WORTH

BACON BRÛLÉE WAFFLE—*BREWED*

Makes 2 servings

Brunch is big in Fort Worth, and this adventurous play on the traditional Belgian waffle comes from one of the coziest, and most tenured, all-day brunch spots in town. Nutella cream sauce, espresso whip, salty bacon, and torched bananas combine for a sweet and savory dish perfect for any time of day.

Note:

A broiler may be used in place of a brûlée torch. Place sugared bananas on a baking sheet under a preheated broiler for approximately 3 minutes until bubbly and browned.

INGREDIENTS

¾ cup heavy cream, divided and chilled

2 tablespoons Nutella® hazelnut spread

2 tablespoons powdered sugar, plus more as needed for dusting

2 tablespoons espresso, chilled (or 1 tablespoon instant espresso)

2 cups prepared storebought waffle batter

4 slices cooked bacon, chopped

2 bananas, sliced lengthwise

¼ cup raw sugar, as needed

2 strawberries, for garnish

DIRECTIONS

1. Warm ¼ cup heavy cream in a small saucepan over low heat. Slowly add Nutella® and whisk until smooth. Remove from heat and set aside. Sauce will continue to thicken as it sets.
2. Add remaining chilled heavy cream to mixing bowl (stainless steel is preferred). Whip with an electric mixer on medium speed for 1 minute. Add powdered sugar and espresso and whip on high speed for 2 to 3 more minutes until stiff peaks have formed. Keep chilled. (May be stored in refrigerator up to 24 hours in advance. For a stronger espresso flavor, another tablespoon may be added.)
3. In a preheated waffle iron, add 1 cup of prepared waffle batter and half of the chopped bacon. Close lid and cook until waffle is golden brown. Repeat for second waffle and keep warm.
4. Sprinkle raw sugar on interior side of sliced bananas. Using a brûlée torch, carefully torch sugared bananas until bubbly and browned. (See note.)
5. To serve, top each waffle with two banana slices and a big dollop of espresso whipped cream. Drizzle waffle with Nutella® sauce. Dust with powdered sugar and garnish with strawberries.

BASIC QUICHE—*THE KIMBELL CAFÉ*

Makes 6-8 servings

The world-renowned Kimbell Art Museum is as popular for its lunch offerings as it is for its stunning exhibitions. Mid-century recipes for soups, sandwiches, salads, and desserts round out the menu, but it's founding chef Shelby Shafer's quiche that sets the bar for any other in town. (See note on filling as this recipe allows for creativity.)

INGREDIENTS

1 (9- to 10-inch) prebaked pie crust

3 large eggs, lightly beaten

1 cup heavy cream

½ cup milk

¼ teaspoon salt

Pinch freshly ground black pepper

¾ cup shredded or crumbled cheese

¾ to 1 cup filling of choice (see note)

½ to 1 teaspoon dried herbs

DIRECTIONS

1. Adjust oven rack to the middle position. Heat oven to 350 degrees.
2. In a bowl, whisk together eggs, cream, milk, salt, and freshly ground black pepper. Set aside.
3. Sprinkle half of the cheese on bottom of crust. Arrange filling and herbs on top of cheese, then top with remaining cheese. Gently pour in egg mixture.
4. Place quiche on a foil-lined baking sheet. Bake for 20 minutes. Rotate for even browning, then continue baking for another 20 to 25 minutes, until mixture is set and lightly browned. Test by inserting knife near the center. When set, the knife will come out clean. Set quiche on a wire rack to cool slightly before cutting.

FILLINGS

Since taking over the Kimbell Café kitchen in 2016, chef Peter Kreidler has honored his predecessor's time-honored recipes while adding unique touches of his own. Among his creative additions include flavorful quiche filling combinations, such as roasted shallot and garlic; corn and green chilies; roasted potato and chive; or roasted garlic, sauteed spinach, and smoked gouda. Kreidler also adds a bit of crumbled bacon to nearly every quiche.

CHOCOLATE CAKE DOUGHNUTS—*FUNKY TOWN DONUTS*

Yield: 12 doughnuts

There are a lot of nicknames for Fort Worth, and "Funky Town"—a nod to the city's eclectic vibe—is near the top. This doughnut recipe from the family-owned Funky Town Donuts serves a good base for lots of funky toppings. Think crushed nuts, cereal, or even candied bacon.

INGREDIENTS

3 cups flour

1 cup sugar

¼ cup cocoa powder

1 tablespoon baking powder

¾ teaspoon baking soda

¼ teaspoon salt

1 teaspoon cinnamon

1 cup buttermilk

4 tablespoons half-and-half

½ teaspoon vanilla extract

canola oil for frying, as needed

DIRECTIONS

1. Mix all dry ingredients together in a large bowl. Add wet ingredients and mix with a spatula until just combined. Do not overmix or doughnuts won't be crumbly. Cover dough and refrigerate for 30 to 45 minutes.
2. Heavily dust a work surface with flour and roll out dough to approximately ½ inch thick. (The dough will be easier to handle when chilled.) Using a doughnut cutter, cut out doughnuts and place them on individual sheets of wax paper for an easier transition to frying.
3. Heat oil to 375 degrees in a large heavy pan or fryer. Fry donuts for about 1 minute per side. Place on cooling rack before glazing with Chocolate Glaze (recipe follows) or desired glaze and toppings.

CHOCOLATE GLAZE

INGREDIENTS

1 ½ cups powdered sugar

4 tablespoons cocoa powder

1 tablespoon plus 1 teaspoon milk

2 teaspoons water

1 teaspoon vanilla extract

DIRECTIONS

Sift together the sugar and cocoa powder in a medium bowl. Slowly stir in the milk, water, and vanilla, a little at a time, to make a smooth, pourable glaze.

"Just Peachy" Peach Streusel & Candied Pecan Ice Cream, MELT Ice Creams
Photo courtesy of Nate Goins

SWEETS

Cowtown wears its sweet tooth on its sleeve—fresh-baked goods are love languages for many in this town. The locally made tartlets, layered cakes, and lavish pies are somewhat like status symbols for certain celebrations. A storebought dessert from a corporate chain? For the food lovers in this city, the notion is offensive. There are too many homegrown establishments here worthy of the extra time and effort to patronize them. Some of Cowtown's finest fall on the pages ahead.

What's unique about desserts in Fort Worth is that many local bakers and food artisans collaborate on flavors and ingredients. For example, one of Sweet Lucys Pies' most popular offerings is a pecan pie infused with locally distilled TX Whiskey. The local pie shop shares the recipe here. Fort Worth born-and-bred Melt Ice Creams constantly features Cowtown ingredients, like locally roasted espresso in its Cup of TX coffee-flavored ice cream. Melt uses locally grown peaches for their "Just Peachy" peach streusel and candied pecan ice cream featured here.

This chapter also includes Texas classics, like Cowboy Cookies—oatmeal-based and dotted with coconut, pecans, and chocolate chips for sustenance—and Texas Sheet Cake, which has a long history in the Lone Star State dating back to the early 20th century. Typically made in a sheet pan using a thin batter of cocoa powder and buttermilk, the cake boasts an irresistible layer of crackly frosting, which is poured while warm and hardens as it cools.

Classic buttermilk pie and fancy chocolate coffee pot de crème round out the recipes in the section, and both make the dessert course worthy of eating first.

BUTTERMILK PIE—*SWISS PASTRY SHOP*

Makes 6-8 servings

A staple dessert of the South, buttermilk pie is sweet and slightly tangy thanks to its namesake ingredient. At Fort Worth's iconic Swiss Pastry Shop, scratch-made pies are a hot seller, especially during the holiday season. Owner and baker Hans Muller, whose dad opened the business in 1973, shares a home version here.

INGREDIENTS

2 ¾ cups sugar

¾ cup all-purpose flour

pinch of salt

1 cup butter (2 sticks), melted

6 large eggs

2 cups buttermilk

dash vanilla extract

1 (9-inch) unbaked Pie Crust (recipe follows)

DIRECTIONS

1. Using a small tabletop mixer, combine sugar, flour, and salt.
2. Add melted butter and blend until smooth, scraping down the sides of the bowl. Add eggs and keep blending, scraping down the sides. Add buttermilk and vanilla and blend until smooth. Keep chilled until ready to bake.
3. Heat oven to 350 degrees.
4. Fill prepared pie crust with buttermilk filling. Bake until center of pie is no longer liquified, but still wiggles, approximately 35 to 40 minutes. Remove from oven and allow pie to completely set before serving.

PIE CRUST

Yield: 2 (9-inch) pie crusts

INGREDIENTS

1 cup butter or margarine (2 sticks), slightly softened

1 cup shortening or lard

1 ¾ cup all-purpose flour

1 tablespoons sugar

pinch salt

just under 1 cup ice water

DIRECTIONS

1. Using a small tabletop mixer, combine all ingredients, except water, and mix until mealy. Slowly add water and mix until incorporated. Do not over mix.
2. Remove from mixer and form into 2 discs. Chill until firm but malleable, about 30 minutes. Roll each to create 2 9-inch pie crusts. (1 disc may be frozen for future use.)

CHOCOLATE COFFEE POT DE CRÈME—
CLAY PIGEON FOOD & DRINK

Makes 6-7 servings

Opened in 2013, Marcas Paslay's fine dining destination has built a loyal following for its fan-favorite dishes, including egg yolk-topped prime beef tartare, grilled bone marrow, house-made pasta, and this rich and luxurious pot de crème dessert. Perfect for a dinner party, the recipe may be made a day in advance.

INGREDIENTS

2 cups heavy cream

½ cup sugar

2 tablespoons ground decaf coffee

¼ pound chocolate discs, 64% cacao

2 egg yolks, whisked together

1 ½ teaspoons unflavored powdered gelatin (see note)

DIRECTIONS

1. Add cream, sugar, and ground decaf coffee to a medium stock pot. Heat to boiling, stirring frequently to prevent scorching. Do not allow to boil over or scorch.
2. Immediately strain cream mixture through a fine stainless steel strainer into a bowl—a chinois is preferred for the smoothest texture. Gradually whisk in chocolate thoroughly, making sure no chocolate is sticking to the bowl. The cream mixture should be approximately 160 degrees. If too cold, gently heat. If too hot, let sit a few minutes to cool down.
3. To temper the egg yolks into the cream mixture, add about a tablespoon at a time of cream into the egg yolks, whisking constantly to prevent scrambling. When yolks are warmed and smooth, add them back into cream mixture, then whisk in powdered gelatin. Transfer mixture into small jars (honey pots are used at Clay Pigeon). Set for at least 4 hours in the refrigerator, preferably overnight.

Note:

Gelatin sheets are typically used in professional kitchens in place of powdered gelatin and provide a smoother texture. Gelatin sheets may be ordered online or found in restaurant supply stores. Use 1 ¼ sheets for this recipe, soaking first in ice water for 10 minutes before wringing out and adding to mixture.

GRANDMOTHER'S TEXAS SHEET CAKE—*CENTRAL MARKET FORT WORTH*

Makes 9 servings

A Texas classic for its moist texture and crackly layer of thin chocolate icing dotted with toasted pecans, this nostalgic cake has been served for generations at everything from birthdays to funerals. Called "Grandmother's," Central Market's version was inspired by an employee's grandmother who made it for holiday gatherings—like many Texas grandmothers do.

INGREDIENTS

¾ cup all-purpose flour

¾ plus 1 tablespoon cup sugar

¼ cup plus 3 tablespoons unsalted butter

1 ½ tablespoons cocoa powder

¼ cup plus 2 tablespoons water

1 egg

3 tablespoons buttermilk

½ teaspoon vanilla extract

½ teaspoon ground cinnamon

½ teaspoon baking soda

DIRECTIONS

1. Heat oven to 325 degrees. Lightly grease a 9 x 9 pan.
2. Mix flour and sugar in a medium bowl and set aside.
3. In a saucepot, melt the butter over low heat. Add cocoa powder and water and bring to a boil. Remove from heat and add to sugar and flour mixture. Add egg, buttermilk, vanilla extract, cinnamon, and baking soda and mix to combine. Pour batter into prepared pan and bake for approximately 25 to 30 minutes until set.
4. Pour Icing (recipe follows) over the cake while both are still warm.

ICING

INGREDIENTS

¼ cup roughly chopped pecans

3 tablespoons unsalted butter

2 tablespoons whole milk

1 tablespoon cocoa powder

½ teaspoon vanilla extract

1 cup plus 3 tablespoons powdered sugar

DIRECTIONS

1. Heat oven to 350 degrees. Toast pecans on a baking sheet for 6 to 8 minutes, being careful not to burn. Remove and set aside to cool.
2. About 5 minutes before cake is done, melt butter over low heat in a small saucepan. Add milk and cocoa and whisk until combined. Add vanilla extract, powdered sugar, and pecans and whisk. Pour over cake while warm.

"JUST PEACHY" PEACH STREUSEL & CANDIED PECAN ICE CREAM—*MELT ICE CREAMS*

Makes 6 servings

It was 2014 when MELT Ice Creams founder Kari Crowe-Seher realized what was missing from Cowtown's culinary scene: premium small batch ice cream. After testing dozens of recipes during dinner parties with friends, Kari launched her brand and now boasts "scoop shops" all over North Texas. Use fresh Texas peaches for her recipe here.

INGREDIENTS

1 ¾ cups heavy cream, divided

¾ cup sugar

⅛ teaspoon salt

1 ¼ cups whole milk

1 cup Peach Jam (recipe follows)

1 ½ teaspoon vanilla extract

1 cup Streusel (recipe follows)

Candied Pecans (recipe follows)

DIRECTIONS

1. For the ice cream base, pour 1 cup heavy cream into a pot and add the sugar and salt. Cook over medium-low heat until steaming, about 170 to 180 degrees. Remove from the heat and add milk and remaining heavy cream. Allow to chill.
2. To make the ice cream, pour chilled ice cream base, Peach Jam, and vanilla extract into an ice cream machine. Freeze per machine's instructions. After the mixture sets to a point when it resembles soft serve (right before the end of the freezing time), add Streusel and Candied Pecans.

PEACH JAM

INGREDIENTS

2 cups very ripe sliced peach meat, unpeeled

⅓ cup sugar

¼ teaspoon salt

DIRECTIONS

Place peaches into a pot with sugar and salt. Cook over medium heat for 20 minutes until peaches break down and the consistency becomes jammy. Pour mixture into a blender and pulse until smooth. Allow to cool before adding to ice cream base.

Photo courtesy of Nate Goins

STREUSEL

INGREDIENTS

⅓ cup rolled oats

¼ cup light brown sugar

3 tablespoons all-purpose flour

¼ teaspoon cinnamon

¼ teaspoon salt

2 tablespoons butter, melted

DIRECTIONS

1. Heat oven to 350 degrees.
2. Place all dry ingredients into a bowl. Pour melted butter over dry ingredients and mix thoroughly. Crumble the mixture onto a cookie sheet and bake for approximately 10 minutes, rotating halfway.
3. Remove from oven and allow to completely cool before breaking into small chunks.

CANDIED PECANS

INGREDIENTS

1 egg, yolk removed

1 tablespoon water

4 ounces (approximately 1 cup) raw pecans, roughly chopped

2 tablespoons sugar

2 tablespoons, plus 2 teaspoons light brown sugar

½ teaspoon pumpkin pie spice

½ teaspoon salt

DIRECTIONS

1. Heat oven to 300 degrees. Line a baking sheet with parchment paper.
2. Add egg white and water to a bowl and whisk until foamy. Add chopped pecans and mix well. Reserve.
3. In a separate bowl, combine remaining ingredients. Toss chopped pecans with dry ingredients until well coated. Spread pecans in a single layer on prepared baking sheet. Bake for 10 to 12 minutes, tossing occasionally to prevent burning. Cool pecans before adding to ice cream base.

TX WHISKEY PECAN PIE—*SWEET LUCY'S PIES*

Makes 6-8 servings

One of Fort Worth's most popular pies is this Southern-inspired classic tinged with a taste of locally distilled TX Whiskey. Sweet Lucy's Pies owner Lindsey Lawing (whose daughter is Sweet Lucy) bakes it year-round due to demand. (Tip: Pick up a premade crust at Sweet Lucy's storefront to make this recipe a real breeze.)

INGREDIENTS

1 cup sugar

3 tablespoons brown sugar

1 teaspoon salt

5 tablespoons unsalted butter, melted

1 cup light corn syrup

3 eggs

¼ cup TX Whiskey

1 cup Texas pecans

1 9-inch Flaky All Butter Crust (recipe follows)

DIRECTIONS

1. Heat oven to 350 degrees.
2. Stir sugar, brown sugar, and salt together in a medium bowl. Mix in melted butter and corn syrup, then whisk in the eggs. Add TX Whiskey and mix until combined.
3. Add pecans to pie crust and pour pie filling over pecans. Bake for 50 to 60 minutes. (Bake time will vary depending on oven. Check the pie at 30-minute mark.) The pie crust should be brown and the filling slightly wobbly in the center. Remove from oven and let set. The pie will continue to cook once out of oven. Store at room temperature for up to 2 days or in refrigerator for up to 4 days.

FLAKY ALL BUTTER CRUST

Yield: 2 (9-inch) pie crusts

INGREDIENTS

2 ½ cups all-purpose flour, plus more for rolling, as needed

1 tablespoon sugar

1 ½ teaspoons salt

1 cup (2 sticks) cold unsalted butter, cut into pieces

4 to 6 tablespoons ice cold water, plus more as needed

DIRECTIONS

1. Stir flour, sugar, and salt together in a medium bowl. Add the butter pieces into the flour mixture and toss to coat. Working quickly, use a pastry blender or your hands to mix the butter into the flour until the mixture is crumbly, being careful not to over mix. (You still want larger pieces of butter in the flour.) If ingredients get too warm, place bowl in the refrigerator for 30 minutes until ingredients are chilled.
2. Add cold water to mixture, 1 tablespoon at a time, until dough comes together. Cut dough in half and form 2 disks. Store 1 in the freezer for another time and 1 in the refrigerator for 30 minutes.
3. Once dough has chilled, roll out on a floured surface using a floured rolling pin. Start rolling from the center of the dough and roll away. Rotate the dough until the entire disk is rolled out. Place dough in desired pie pan and crimp edges.

Photo courtesy of Lauren Cook

COWBOY COOKIES— *CAST IRON AT OMNI FORT WORTH HOTEL*

Yield: approximately 4 dozen

You don't have to be a real cowboy to saddle up for these satisfying sweet treats, which are studded with a trifecta of coconut, pecans, and chocolate. Said to be named for keeping cowboys' hunger at bay on the range, Cast Iron's version is fit for a modern-day rodeo champ.

INGREDIENTS

⅔ cup butter (1 ⅓ sticks), softened

½ cup coconut oil, solidified

¾ cup sugar

1 cup plus 1 tablespoon brown sugar, packed

3 eggs, room temperature

2 teaspoons vanilla extract

2 ¼ cups all-purpose flour

2 ½ cups instant steel cut oats

1 ½ teaspoons baking soda

1 ½ teaspoons ground cinnamon

1 teaspoon salt

1 ½ cups semi-sweet chocolate chips

1 ½ cups pecans, chopped

2 cups shredded sweetened coconut

DIRECTIONS

1. Heat oven to 350 degrees. Line 2 baking sheets with parchment paper.
2. Using an electric mixer on medium speed, cream the butter, coconut oil and sugar in a large bowl until light and fluffy. Slowly add eggs and vanilla while still mixing. Set aside.
3. Combine all dry ingredients in a separate large bowl. Slowly add dry ingredients to wet ingredients using a spatula until just combined. Fold in chocolate chips, pecans, and coconut.
4. Using a spoon or ice cream scooper, drop small cookie dough scoops onto baking sheets at least 2 inches apart. Bake for 12 to 15 minutes until golden brown around the edges.

INDEX